D0891938

DISCARD

SHAMBHALA LIBRARY

The Poetry of Zen

Edited and translated by

SAM HAMILL
and
J. P. SEATON

SHAMBHALA
CPL Boston & London
2004

FRONTISPIECE: Kanzan and Jittoku by Gako (Tengen Chiben, 1737-1805). Private Collection.

Translation of the inscription:

> My heart is like the autumn moon,
> Pure and unsullied on the blue-green pool.

SHAMBHALA PUBLICATIONS, INC.
Horticultural Hall
300 Massachusetts Avenue
Boston, Massachusetts 02115
www.shambhala.com

9 8 7 6 5 4 3 2 1

PRINTED IN CHINA
♾ This edition is printed on acid-free paper that meets the American National Standards Institute z39.48 Standard. Distributed in the United States by Random House, Inc., and in Canada by Random House of Canada Ltd

Library of Congress Cataloging-in-Publication Data
The poetry of Zen/edited and translated by Sam Hamill and J.P. Seaton
—1st ed.
p. cm.
ISBN 1-57062-863-7 (hardcover: alk paper)
1. Zen poetry, Japanese—Translations into English.
2. Zen poetry, Chinese—Translations into English.
I. Hamille, Sam. II. Seaton, Jerome P.
PL782.E3P624 2004
895.6′1080382943927—dc22   CIP
2004002480

CONTENTS

Contents

PART TWO: JAPANESE POEMS
*Introduction to the Japanese
Poems by Sam Hamill* 91

Contents

The Poetry of Zen

PREFACE

"ZEN IS A MATTER OF CHARACTER, not a matter of intellect," as D. T. Suzuki emphasized. And yet there are probably tens of thousands of readers of Zen books for every one who has experienced Zen, which means simply, "meditative absorption." Its practice, its embodiment, is *zazen* (*tso-ch'an* in Chinese), "sitting meditation." Without a daily sitting practice, the experience of Zen remains an intellectual exercise. Only through maintaining such a practice may one begin to encounter the true "collectedness of mind and compassionate heart" that leads to self-realization and transcendent wisdom.

When D. T. Suzuki stressed character over intellect three-quarters of a century ago, there were very few books on Zen available in English. The great Zen teachers and poets of China and Japan were virtually unknown in the West, and the term itself remained largely obscure until the San Francisco Renaissance of the 1950s, when Jack Kerouac's novel *The Dharma Bums* and the poetry and essays of Kenneth Rexroth, Gary Snyder, Philip Whalen, and Alan Watts brought it to public attention. Despite his eccentric and often

I

wrongheaded notions of Buddhism in general and Zen in particular, Jack Kerouac introduced the eighth-century Chinese poet Han Shan ("Cold Mountain") to tens of thousands of readers, and although he referred to them by pseudonyms, he helped also introduce readers to poets Gary Snyder and Philip Whalen.

Since its inception, Zen has had a paradoxical relationship with literature, especially as regards translation and poetry. The practice of translating was born with the teachings of Siddhartha Gautama, known as Shakyamuni Buddha (sixth century BCE), a title meaning "Awakened Sage of the Shakya Clan." The Buddha asked his disciples to translate his teachings into all the languages and dialects of his native India. Those teachings (sutras) contained allegorical tales, anecdotes, recorded conversations, and ritual verses. Even at the beginning of Buddhism, poetry was an essential aid to understanding.

The most influential sutra in the world of Zen, Hui Neng's early T'ang dynasty (seventh century) *Platform Sutra* declares: "The complete teachings of all Buddhas—past, present and future—are to be found within the essence of every human being." Hui Neng was an illiterate woodcutter, but his insights were persuasively penetrating. He believed that only those who could not grasp that "essence" needed teachers. He advocated *shikantaza,* just *sitting,* which he defined as a meditative state in which perception is utterly free of discrimination between mind and matter, self and object; where the only permanence is impermanence; and where change, whether subtle or violent, remains the essence of being. He suggested that the practice itself is an expression of enlightenment and therefore leads to ever greater enlightenment. "Realizing one's own real essence is the ultimate expression of enlightenment." In short, Hui Neng's Zen stripped away the rituals, lineages, and formalities that had become a cumbersome institution in Chinese Buddhist traditions.

Zen practice is eminently simple and profoundly rigorous. All the questions of being are called forth. There is no escape into faith. "In your heart, you already know." The tenth-century Zen master Penhsien reminded his followers not to depend too much on sutras or *kōan* study. "If you really want to get to the truth of Zen, get it while walking, while standing, while sleeping or sitting ... while working." Only then, he says, can one begin to define what doctrines are actually being followed.

While stressing one kind of nonjudgmental perception, Zen masters often express severe and unsettling judgments. D. T. Suzuki wrote, "When Buddhists are told that the Buddha comes from nowhence and departs no-whither ... they are at a loss, or they try to snap at empty space, imagining that this may lead them somewhere. But they will never wake up to [Zen] until their nose is twisted hard and tears come from their eyes."

In the thirteenth century, Ch'ih-chueh observed, "The failure of the Zen path comes from teachers without deep attainment just setting forth sayings and showing off knowledge to capture students, and from students with no great aspiration just following popular fads and current customs, content to sink themselves in the domain of intellectual knowledge and verbiage. . . . The 'teachers' and 'students' bewitch each other." As regards "verbiage," Yueh-lin observed, "Ninety percent accuracy is not as good as silence."

If the essence of Zen is not to be found in words, why so much poetry in the Zen tradition? The use of poetry goes back to the very roots of Indian traditions, as well as to Chinese roots. In the birth of Zen, two poems play a particularly important role. Shen-hsiu, the great Ch'an master of the Northern school, wrote a verse:

> This body is the Bodhi tree.
> The mind is like a bright mirror.
> Polish it and keep it clean,
> let no dust mote settle there.

Hui Neng wrote a verse in reply:

> There is no Bodhi tree.
> No bright mirror exists.

Since all is emptiness,
where could a dust mote settle?

Poetry often says what cannot be said in prose. It was used for argument, description, ceremony, memorialization, and some were even *kōans*—"cases" for meditation. Poetry is most capable of capturing the essence of a moment's experience. Ninety-nine percent accuracy in poetry is not as good as silence. A good poem says more than the sum of its words, leading the reader into the practice of understanding the great unsaid that is contained, framed in a poem's rhythms, words, and silences. In these ways, poetry opens the mind. "The mind is Buddha!" Hui Neng declares. All of this makes poetry an excellent aid to practice. The same might be said of poetry in the Bible.

J. P. Seaton and I have surveyed the broad lay tradition of Zen poetry, including in this anthology samples of the Zen influence on the poetry of major Chinese and Japanese poets not often associated formally with Zen institutions, or even Zen practice. China's greatest poet, Tu Fu, is usually classified as a Confucian, but in certain of his poems, the Zen essence is expressed elegantly and succinctly. He, like most Chinese, lived and thought through the *san-chiao,* three systems (Taoism, Confucianism, and Buddhism), and often one aspect outshines the others within a single poem. The world's most famous Zen poet, the T'ang dynasty's legendary Han Shan, was a ragged beggar who scratched poems on the cave walls where he lived and who worked as a helper in the kitchen of a Zen monastery.

The most influential poet in the history of Zen poetry in Japan is Saigyō, a monk of the Shingon, or "True Speech," school of Buddhism. He accurately predicted, years in advance, that he would die on the same calendar day as that on which Shakyamuni Buddha had died, and his poetry deeply embodies the spirit of Zen, celebrating not the self or seer, but the world seen. He made *sabi* ("aloneness") and *sabishisa* ("loneliness") essential elements in the Japanese tradition of Zen poetry. He was a major inspiration for such poets as Bashō, Issa, and Ryōkan.

Monks and lay poets together are the heart and mind of the Zen poetic tradition. Their influence can be seen in the works of many contemporary American writers, from renowned poets such as Gary Snyder, Allen Ginsberg, Kenneth Rexroth, W. S. Merwin, and Jane Hirshfield, to poets not generally associated with Buddhism, like Denise Levertov, Robert Hass, Jim Harrison, and Hayden Carruth. In America, Zen and Zen poetry is as American as apple pie. There is nothing intrinsically Chinese, Japanese, Indian, or Korean about Zen beyond its Chinese roots. Its institutions sometimes wear the cultural accoutrements of their countries, but the practice transcends any such distinctions.

Preface

Our anthology is but a sampling of a long, noble tradition. We follow a long line of Bud-dhist/Taoist translators who struggled to follow the path that is most simple, yet profoundly difficult. Poetry, we believe—as Hui Neng and Shakyamuni before him believed—is one of the many paths to enlightenment. It is no substitute for *zazen*, but an aid to deepen one's practice day by day. Zen poetry is about character.

S.H.

PART ONE

Chinese Poems

Introduction
to the Chinese Poems

Z EN IS TAOIST BUDDHISM. Or: Zen is Buddhist
Taoism: at least when talking about Ch'an, the
Chinese version of Zen, the ancestor of the Japanese,
Korean, Vietnamese, and the various evolving West-
ern versions of this branch of Buddhist practice. The
association of Ch'an with the arts, from the *martial*
arts, as in hand-to-hand combat and archery, to the
powerful *civil* arts of poetry and painting, begins in
China, from the association of these arts with the
Taoist practice of meditation and the Taoist emphasis
on *wei-wu-wei*, doing non-doing, doing without
doing, or doing, through practice and concentration,
with total freedom and absolute creativity.

Maybe to the dismay of newcomers to American
Buddhism who expect a pure and fundamentalist
Zen, of one particular school or another (like the
Rinzai and Soto sects of Japan, which have been ar-
guing for several centuries over whether the *kōan*
should be central to Zen meditation practice), we
start our selection of Ch'an poems with excerpts
from the Taoist book *Tao Te Ching* of Lao Tzu, a book

known to orthodox Ch'an men like Han Shan (now there's a fundamentalist!) as "The Five Thousand Character Classic" or "The Five Thousand Words." Lao Tzu's insights and his penchant for putting them into verse are certainly two sources of the Ch'an stream.

We bow in thanks first not to poets themselves, but to the monk-translators who came to their work of translating the holy books of Buddhism from their original Indian languages into Chinese from a background in Taoist philosophy and poetic art. Our first Ch'an poet, Hui Yung, although he wrote nearly a thousand years after Lao Tzu, must technically also be pre-Ch'an, since he died more than a hundred years before the purported arrival in China of the first patriarch of Ch'an, the Indian monk Bodhidharma. As a translator, Hui Yung favored the practice of translating Buddhist terminology from the Sanskrit, wherever possible, with preexisting Taoist terms. Another school of translators preferred to render these in "transliteration" only. Hui Yung's approach brought many educated laypeople immediately into contact with Buddhist thought, and began the process of making Buddhist ideas comfortably Chinese.

Hui Yung was an active and effective missionary: with his better-known brother, the monk-translator Hui Yuan, he promoted a famous association of lay Buddhist practitioners called the White Lotus Society, whose members pledged to support the Buddhist ideal of universal compassion, and who met regularly to discuss philosophy, sit in meditation, and probably write poetry, without formally becoming Buddhist monks. In China, where continuing the family line with male children was a nearly sacred duty, and family life, as well as sex itself, was a recognized pleasure, the vow of celibacy taken by monks was a particularly strong bar for upper-class men to formal affiliation with Buddhism. Hui Yung's opening of practice to non-monks was a masterstroke of missionary policy.

Our first non-monk poet, T'ao Ch'ien, acknowledged as among the greatest of all classical Chinese poets, declined to join the White Lotus Society, even after a personal invitation from Hui Yuan, which came accompanied by a dispensation of the society's rule against drinking, T'ao Ch'ien's lifelong vice. T'ao is known as a Taoist. We agree with Hui Yuan and Hui Yung: he's a Buddhist Taoist, or a Taoist Buddhist. What's Zen enough for Hui Yuan is Zen enough for our anthology. Doctrinal lines are blurred in quite a few other places, too. From T'ao Ch'ien on, the selection is sprinkled with lay and clerical poets.

Hsieh Ling-yun is, like T'ao, famous as a poet of nature. He was an aristocrat with strong Buddhist leanings. Wang Fan-chih, like the legendary pair of madmen, Han Shan and Shih Te, was a ragged wanderer. It is quite possible that none of these three ever officially joined a monastery, even though Han Shan and Shih Te worked in the kitchen of the famous Tien-t'ai monastery and are celebrated in Ch'an as reincarnations of the Indian bodhisattvas Manjushri and Samantabhadra. Ironically, the Manchu Ch'ing dynasty emperors also claimed to be Manjushri in order to outrank the then-current reincarnation of the Dalai Lama. Clearly, when dealing with the history of Ch'an, we are dealing not only with enlightened men and women, but with a human institution as well.

The T'ang dynasty was in many ways a high point for Buddhism in China, and Ch'an was truly born, in the eighth century, as a separate school of Tien-t'ai Buddhism. The dynasty is also known as the golden age of Chinese poetry, and many Ch'an monks made use of poetry both as artistic practice and as a means of teaching, "by direct pointing." The attraction of lay poets to Ch'an themes, and the social and poetic interaction of even the most committedly secular of the Confucian lay poets with monks and monk-poets, make it clear that the flourishing of both traditions was certainly a mutually nourishing phenomenon. The T'ang lay poets show the broad range and variety of influence of Zen among the educated elite. They shared a serious commitment to Zen meditation practice, and the influence of Zen's apparently paradoxical view that enlightenment is illusion, and illusion enlightenment. (*"Nirvana* is *samsara* and *samsara* is *nirvana.*")

Li Po, though a legendary drinker, was also a committed meditator. Tu Fu, a Confucian official and family man par excellence, was a devotee of T'ien-t'ai Buddhism, and an open admirer of the new "sect." Wang Wei, the third in the triumvirate of the "greatest" of the High T'ang poets, was an aristocrat who became a high Confucian official. He was also a patron of Ch'an monks and monasteries and one of the people in the lay world most responsible for the growth and popularity of Hui Neng's version of Ch'an (as the "Southern school," the progenitor, through Hui Neng's five main disciples, of the major wings of Ch'an, including those that flew to Japan to become the Soto and Rinzai sects).

Others have greater and lesser links to Ch'an. Po Chu-i, certainly one of the greatest of the great, worried that his poems represented a karmic "attachment" that he was unable to break. He wrote about ten thousand poems. Tu Mu, a late T'ang master of the quatrain, bragged at once ironically and clearly ruefully, of how his lustful nature had earned him fame as a "heartless man," and how his lust for fame and power had kept him from knowing his own children. Though his self-mockery is clear, his "attachments" to both poetry and Ch'an are, paradoxically, clear as well.

Of the T'ang monks whose work is included here, four, Hsuan Chueh, Chiao Jan, Wu Pen (better known by his lay name, Chia Tao), and Kuan Hsiu offer examples of the wide variety of approaches to life and to poetry present even among the monk-poets. Clearly, in T'ang China, where Ch'an (and Zen) began, it was a living tradition, unbound by doctrine and dogma. This was the period when the great teachers still used *wenda* (Japanese *mondo*), face-to-face question and answer, dialogic teaching like the Socratic method. The period before these creative personal interactions had been codified into *kung-an* (Japanese *kōan*), "case examples" for study and meditation, to be followed by examinations by the abbot or resident master.

Direct pointing by another human was an important adjunct to "sitting," or *zazen* practice. T'ang was a period in which it was expected that young Ch'an searchers would go from temple to temple looking for a master to match their own personalities, their own ways of learning. When Chia Tao speaks to a friend of "masterless Ch'an, our own understanding," he is not voicing a heresy. On the other hand, the monk Hsuan Chueh was disciple and "dharma heir" of Hui Neng, who is credited with giving Ch'an its unique form as a separate branch of T'ien-t'ai Buddhism. Our selection of Hsuan Chueh's poems is from a longer work, *Cheng Tao Ko* "Canticle of the Way"), that is sometimes taken as a whole by later generations of Zennists who study it as a holy text.

Among the monk-poets, the aristocratic Chiao Jan, a friend of the great lay poets of the high T'ang, was also one of the first of the Ch'an monks to find poetry itself an "attachment" to the world of *samsara* that he felt he must, in the end, also give up. He may have set the model that the layman Po Chu-i *tried* to follow. Chiao Jan's poems have the beauty and serenity we might cynically expect from a "well-placed" monk, but they can also be surprisingly iconoclastic.

Chia Tao entered a Ch'an monastery at an early age, probably taken in as an orphan in the turbulent times of the eighth century. He too succumbed to the poetry demon that worried both the monk Chiao Jan and the layman Po Chu-i. A large selection of the poems he wrote as a monk, under the name Wu Pen, is included in the forty volume Ch'ing Dynasty compilation, *Chuan T'ang Shih* ("Complete Poems of the T'ang"). When his poetry caused him to be recognized by the great anti-Buddhist Confucian official Han Yu, he gave up holy orders, grew back his hair, took up a minor office in the government, and wrote a lot more great poetry. Qualifying this apostasy were the facts that the Ch'an oath is to save all sentient beings from suffering, and that people were suffering most from bad government. Moreover, his patron Han Yu was a great reformer and a gifted and inventive poet.

The monk-poet-painter Kuan Hsiu can be seen as fulfilling the prophecy of Chia Tao's lifestyle in an even more tumultuous period of history. Like Chia

Tao, he probably escaped starvation as a child when taken in by a Buddhist orphanage. During and after the collapse of the T'ang, he spent his life traveling from the territory of one petty tyrant's tiny regional regime to another, much like the Confucius of the Spring and Autumn period, looking for a lord of sufficient intellectual and ethical power to absorb his political teaching: "If you stop eating the people, and offer them security instead, you may make yourself emperor of all China." He found no takers for his political advice, but he did manage to become proclaimed the greatest poet of his age. His poem "Bad Government" shows his political candor at its clearest. Written in popular ballad style, using colloquial language and mocking puns, it reaches for the hearts and minds of common people. Indeed, the powerful colloquial language of most of his work influenced the best of the Sung dynasty poets, clerical and lay alike.

The T'ang poets, monks and laymen alike, threw open the gates for those who followed. Su Tung-p'o of the Sung dynasty is one of the greatest of all Chinese poets, acclaimed for, among many things, his inspired use of ordinary spoken language. Both Po Chu-i and Kuan Hsiu may have served as his models. Zennists claim him as a Ch'an man, and cite his "enlightenment poem" (see page 73, *To the Abbot of the Tung-lin Monastery*), although he remained a layman throughout his long and often difficult life, and pointedly refused Buddhist last rites.

Some might argue that Yuan Mei, the greatest lay poet of the Ch'ing dynasty, wasn't Zen at all, but by the Ch'ing, all educated men with good minds were acquainted with Ch'an, and most were well-disposed to its teachings. Yuan Mei appreciated and understood Ch'an, obviously, and practiced meditation. And if he said, "I Don't Bow to Buddhas," (the title I took for my translations of selected poems of Yuan Mei) in one poem, he added, in the same poem, "but I do bow to a monk." Yuan's favorite "Confucian" was Wang Yang-ming, the Neo-Confucian most popular among disaffected intellectuals like Yuan, and among the anti-Manchu Chinese nationalist secret societies of the eighteenth and nineteenth century, was damned as a heretic by "orthodox" Confucians and accused specifically of being a "follower of Ch'an."

Ching An, writing a century after Yuan Mei, was a powerful abbot who lived to fight, without much success, for the protection of the Buddhist cultural heritage after the end of the final dynasty, the Ch'ing, in the early years of the twentieth century. He was also esteemed by the best lay poets of his period.

The final poet represented in this anthology, Po Ching, is better known by his lay name, Su Man-shu. He was the son of a Chinese merchant and a Japanese mother and bought or stole his monk's certificate. He also worked hard for the revitalization of Buddhism by writing the first Sanskrit grammar in

Chinese. Interestingly, one of the last great traditional poets, Liu Ya-tzu, who commissioned his own son, Liu Wu-chi, to edit Su's works for publication after the poet's early death, was also Chairman Mao's editor, or ghost writer, depending on to whom one listens.

Would any sect or church in the world but Ch'an tolerate them all, much less welcome them? And yet they teach us friendship and a clear-headedness that transcends the ages. They strengthen our character.

Lao Tzu
(4TH CENTURY BCE)

Tao Te Ching

I

Tao defined is not the constant Tao.
No name names its eternal name.

The unnamable is the origin of heaven and earth;
named, it is the mother of the ten thousand things.

Emptied of desire, we see the mystery;
filled with desire, we see the manifestation of
    things.

Two names emerge from a single origin,
and both are called mysterious,

and the mystery itself is the gateway to perception.

[S.H.]

2

BEAUTY and ugliness have one origin.
Name beauty, and ugliness is.
Recognizing virtue recognizes evil.

Is and *is not* produce one another.
The difficult is born in the easy,
long is defined by short, the high by the low.
Instrument and voice achieve one harmony.
Before and *after* have places.

That is why the sage can act without effort
and teach without words,
nurture things without possessing them,
and accomplish things without expecting merit:

only one who makes no attempt to possess it
cannot lose it.

[S.H.]

7

HEAVEN is eternal. The earth endures.

The reason for heaven's eternity and earth's
    endurance
is that they do not live for themselves only,
and therefore may live forever.

The sage steps back but remains in front,
the outsider always within.

Self is realized through selflessness.

[S.H.]

T'ao Ch'ien

(365–427)

Drinking Alone in the Rainy Season

Whatever lives must meet its end—
that is the way it has always been.

If Taoist immortals were once alive,
where are they today?

The old man who gave me wine
claimed it was the wine of the immortals.

One small cup and a thousand worries vanish;
two, and you'll even forget about heaven.

But is heaven really so far away?
It is best to trust in the Tao.

A crane in the clouds has magic wings
to cross the earth in a moment.

It's been forty years of struggle
since I first became reclusive.

Now that my body is nearly dead,
my heart is pure. What more is there to say?

[S.H.]

HSIEH LING-YUN

(385–433)

Visiting Pai-an Pavilion

BESIDE this dike, I shake off the world's dust,
enjoying walks alone near my brushwood house.

A small stream gurgles down a rocky gorge.
Mountains rise beyond the trees,

kingfisher blue, almost beyond description,
but reminding me of the fisherman's simple life.

From a grassy bank, I listen
as springtime fills my heart.

Finches call and answer in the oaks.
Deer cry out, then return to munching weeds.

I remember men who knew a hundred sorrows,
and the gratitude they felt for gifts.

Joys and sorrows pass, each by each,
failure at one moment, happy success the next.

But not for me. I have chosen freedom
from the world's cares. I chose simplicity.

[S.H.]

Written on the Lake While Returning to Stone Cliff Hermitage

Dawn to dusk, the weather constantly changed,
mountain and lake sometimes vibrant in sunlight,

bright sunlight that made me so happy
I forgot about going home.

Leaving the valley at daybreak,
I didn't disembark until dusk,

forest and gorge clothed in shadows,
sunset clouds melting into evening mist.

There were water chestnuts and lotus,
cattails and rushes growing thickly.

I had to push them aside to pass southward,
happy to be reaching my home in the east.

When the mind stops striving, the world's not a
    problem.
A constant heart won't waver from the truth.

A few words to nurture the living, to say:
follow this teaching if you want to know the way.

[S.H.]

Hui Yung

(4TH–5TH CENTURY)

Translating Holy Books

WE go unwinding the woof
from the web of meaning.

Words of the sutras
day by day come forth.

Head on, we chase the mystery of the dharma.

[J.P.S.]

Moon Sitting

ON this high froth-tipped mountain,
the temple owns few lamps.
Sit facing the moon's glitter.
Out of season, heart of ice.

[J.P.S.]

WANG FAN-CHIH

(590–660)

Two Untitled Poems

THE city wall's the noodle dumpling,
What's inside's just the meatball.

One each, and don't complain
about the flavor.

[J.P.S.]

WHEN the rich pass proudly by
on big, smooth horses,
I feel foolish
riding my scrawny donkey.

I feel much better
when we overtake
a bundle of sticks
riding a bony man.

[S.H.]

Hsuan Chueh

(665–713)

From *Canticle of the Way*

Heart's mirror clear reflects beyond fetter. .
The void stripped clean, innumerable worlds.

All things in their majesty, shadowed and seen
   there.
The single gleaming jewel: not within, not without.

[J.P.S.]

∾

One moon seen as one in all the waters.
All waters' moon, that one moon holds.

Thus, the Buddha-dharma in my being:
my being at one with the Awakened One.

[J.P.S./S.H.]

Han Shan

(8th century)

1

Pigs eat the flesh of dead men.
Men dine on dead pigs.
Pigs don't mind the stink of man.
But if a pig just dies, people throw it in the water.
And if a man dies, he's buried out of sight.
Then they lose interest in each other.
Yet the Buddha's lotus is born in boiling water.

[J.P.S./S.H.]

2

I stand here and watch the people of this world:
all against one and one against all,
angry, arguing, plotting and scheming.
Then one day, suddenly, they die.
And each gets one plot of ground:
four feet wide, six feet long.
If you can scheme your way out of that plot,
I'll set the stone that immortalizes your name.

[J.P.S.]

3

Human beings live in the dirt,
like bugs in a filthy bowl.
All day long crawling around and around,
never getting over the edge.

Even spiritual masters can't make it,
wracking their brains for schemes and plans.
The months and the years, a running river:
Then there's the day you wake up old.

[J.P.S.]

4

Parrots live in the western lands.
Forest hunters net them and bring them here.
Courtesans love to play with them, and so
they are well known at court, in and out all day.

They're given golden cages to dwell in,
but bolted in, their robes of plumes are ruined.
Better a swan, or a crane . . . riding the winds
high up, well known to the clouds where they fly.

[J.P.S.]

5

Mr. Wang's degree says Flourishing Talent.
He loves to find fault with my poems.

He says I don't follow the regulations,
and don't use the right techniques.

He says I don't use the four tones correctly,
and just stick in words any which way.

I laugh at what he calls poetry: a blind man's
rhymes in lukewarm praise of the sun.

[J.P.S.]

6

My heart's like the autumn moon,
reflecting from the clear pure waters of the pool.
There's nothing to compare:
What can I say?

[J.P.S.]

7

THE gorge is long, rocks, and rocks and rocks,
  jut up,
The torrent's wide, reeds almost hide the other side.
The moss is slippery even without rain.
The pines sing; the wind is real enough.
Who's ready to leap free of the world's traces:
come sit with me among white clouds?

[J.P.S.]

8

EAST of me, the old lady
Got rich three or four years ago.
Used to be poorer than me,
Now she laughs that I don't have money.
She laughs that I've fallen behind.
I laugh that she's gotten ahead.
Both of us laughing, no stopping us.
East, and West.

[J.P.S.]

9

IDLY, I wander to the flowering peak.
Morning sun: its glory blazing
All around, in sunlit emptiness
White clouds, and cranes, fly.

[J.P.S.]

10

JADE green pool spring water's clear.
The spirit of itself brings dark mysteries to light.
Meditate on emptiness: it's all the more quiet.

[J.P.S.]

Shih Te

(8th Century)

Five Poems

You say, "If you want to be happy
there's no way, but to be a hermit.
Flowers in the grove are better than brocade,
every single season's colors new.
Just sit by a creek and turn your head
to watch the moon's ball roll."
And me? I ought to be at joyous ease,
but I can't help thinking of the people in the world.

[J.P.S.]

W HEN I was young I studied books and
    swordsmanship,
and rode off with a shout to the Capital,
where, I heard, the barbarians had been driven off
    already . . .
there was no place left for heroes.
So I came back to these crested peaks,
lay down and listened to the clear stream flow.
Young men dream of glory:
monkeys riding on the ox's back.

[J.P.S.]

I 'VE always been Shih Te, the Foundling.
It's not some accidental title.
Yet I'm not without a family.
Han Shan is my brother,
two men with hearts a lot alike.
No need for vulgar love.
If you want to know how old we are . . .
like the Yellow River, that's unclear.

[J.P.S.]

You want to learn to catch a mouse?
Don't try to learn from a pampered cat.
If you want to learn the nature of the world,
don't study fine bound books.
The True Jewel's in a coarse bag.
Buddha-nature stops at huts.
The whole herd of folks who clutch at looks of
    things
never seem to make the connection.

[J.P.S.]

My poems are poems;
some people call them sermons.
Well, poems and sermons share one thing:
when you read them you've got to be careful.
Keep at it. Get into detail.
Don't just claim they're easy.
If you were to live your life like that,
a lot of funny things might happen.

[J.P.S.]

MENG HAO-JAN
(689–740)

Master I's Chamber in the Ta-yu Temple

I-KUNG's place to practice Ch'an:
a hut in an empty grove.

Outside the door, a single pretty peak.
Before the stair, deep valleys.

Sunset confused in footprints of the rain.
Blue of the void in the shade of the court.

Look, and see the lotus blossom's purity:
know then that nothing taints this heart.

[J.P.S.]

Spring Dreams

IN spring, I dream through dawn,
but hear birds everywhere, singing.

O voice of all-night wind and rain,
do you count the petals that are falling?

[S.H.]

A Night on the River

MOORED in island mist,
as the sun sets, a traveler's grief arises.

Beyond the great plain, the sky closes on trees.
On this gentle river, the moon arrives.

[S.H.]

WANG CH'ANG-LING
(698–756)

In the Company of a Monk

PALM blossoms fill the court.
Moss grows in the empty room.

All conversation done,
in emptiness, sensing a strange fragrance.

[J.P.S.]

Li Po

(701–762)

Questions Answered

You ask why I live
alone in the mountain forest,

and I smile and am silent
until even my soul grows quiet.

The peach trees blossom.
The water continues to flow.

I live in the other world,
one that lies beyond the human.

[S.H.]

Old Dust

WE live our lives as wanderers
until, dead, we finally come home.

One quick trip between heaven and earth,
then the dust of a thousand generations.

The Moon Rabbit mixes elixirs for nothing.
The Tree of Long Life is kindling.

Dead, our white bones lie silent
when pine trees lean toward spring.

Remembering, I sigh; looking ahead, I sigh once
    more:
This life is mist. What fame? What glory?

[S.H.]

Zazen on Ching-t'ing Mountain

THE birds have vanished from the sky.
Now the last cloud drains away.

We sit together, the mountain and me,
until only the mountain remains.

[S.H.]

42

WANG WEI
(701–761)

Visiting the Mountain Hermitage of a
Monk at Gan-hua Monastery

HE waits as at dusk, bamboo walking stick in hand,
at the headwaters of Tiger Creek,
leading us on as we listen to mountain echoes,
following the water's way.

Patches of wildflowers bloom.
A solitary bird calls from the valley floor.
We sit evening zazen in the empty forest:
quiet pine winds bring the scent of autumn.

[S.H.]

Passing Hsiang-chi Temple

OBLIVIOUS, I pass Hsiang-chi Temple,
walking on through mountain clouds,
an empty trail through ancient trees.
Deep in the mountains, a bell resounds.

The susurrus river flows among stones.
Sunlight streams through frozen pines.
In this still pool, in falling light,
Zen overcomes the serpents of delusion.

[S.H.]

The Way to the Temple

SEARCHING for Gathered Fragrance Temple:
miles of mountains rise into clouds,
ancient trees darken the narrow trail.
Where is that mountain temple bell?

Snowmelt crashes down on boulders,
the sun grows cold in the pines before
it drowns in the lake. Keep your karma
in good working order: many dragons lie in wait.

[S.H.]

Crossing the Yellow River

A LITTLE boat on the great river
whose waves reach the end of the sky—

suddenly a great city, ten thousand
houses dividing sky from wave.

Between the towns there are
hemp and mulberry trees in the wilds.

Look back on the old country:
wide waters; clouds; and rising mist.

[S.H.]

To Magistrate Chang

LATE, I love but quietness:
things of this world are no more my concern.
Looking back, I've known no better plan
than this: returning to the grove.

Pine breezes loosen my robe.
Mountain moonbeams play my lute.
What, you ask, is Final Truth?
The fisherman's song strikes deep into the bank.

[J.P.S.]

CH'ANG CHIEN
(708–765?)

At the P'o-shan Monastery

CLEAR dawn enters the ancient temple.
First sun brightens the lofty grove.
Winding paths lead off to secret places.
Ch'an chamber: flowers deep among the trees.

In mountain light, singing joy is bird-nature.
Pool shadows: empty, the hearts of men.
All sounds here fall to silence.
All that remains: the bell-stone's tone.

[J.P.S.]

Liu Ch'ang-ch'ing
(710–785?)

Searching for the Taoist Monk Ch'ang at South Creek

THE way is crossed by many paths,
the moss by sandal tracks.
White clouds lean, at rest on the silent island.
Fragrant grasses bar the idle gate.

Rain past, observe the color of the pines.
Out along the mountain, to the source,
flowers in the stream reveal Ch'an's meaning:
face-to-face, all words gone.

[J.P.S.]

Bidding Farewell to a Monk

FROM Bamboo Forest Temple,
I faintly hear the evening bell.

Twilight touches the brim of your hat
as you turn and enter dark blue hills.

[S.H.]

Tu Fu
(712–770)

Visiting the Monastery at Lung-men

I EXPLORED the grounds with monks this
evening,
and now the night has passed.

Heavy silence rises all around us
while late moonlight spills through the forest.

The mountain rises almost into heaven.
Sleeping in the clouds is cold.

A single stroke of the early prayer-bell wakes me.
Does it also waken my soul?

[S.H.]

I Stand Alone

A FALCON hovers at the edge of the sky.
Two gulls drift slowly up the river.

Vulnerable while they ride the wind,
they coast and glide with ease.

Dew is heavy on the grass below,
the spider's web is ready.

Heaven's ways include the human:
among a thousand sorrows, I stand alone.

[S.H.]

Clear After Rain

LONG after rainfall, Sorceress Hills grow dark.
Now they brighten, stitched with gold and silver.

Green grass edges the darkening lake
and red clouds stream from the east.

All day long, the orioles call,
and cranes brush tall white clouds.

Once dry, the wildflowers bend and, there
where the wind is sweeping, fall.

[S.H.]

Moon, Rain, Riverbank

RAIN roared through, now
the autumn night is clear.
The water wears a patina of gold
and carries a bright jade star.
Heavenly River runs clear and pure,
as gently as before.

Sunset buries the mountains in shadow.
A mirror floats in the deep green void,
its light reflecting the cold, wet dusk,
dew glistening,
freezing on the flowers.

[S.H.]

Night Thoughts While Traveling

THIN grass bends on the breezy shore,
and the tall mast seems lonely in my boat.

Stars wide low across the wide plain,
and the moon is tossed by the Yangtze.

What is fame and literary status?
The old and infirm should leave office.

Adrift, drifting: what is left for the lone gull
adrift between earth and heaven.

[S.H.]

Ch'ien Ch'i

(722–780)

Gazing from High on the Mountain in the Rainy Season and Thinking of the Monks in the Yu-lin Monastery

From the mountain, rain upon the misty sea,
dripping foam from these misty trees.
It looks as if in that vastness
those dark isles might any moment fly away.
Nature has angered the eight-headed spirit of
    the sea.
The rushing tides stir up the road of the clouds.
The true men fill my thoughts,
but a single reed can't float across.

Sad thoughts of the times at Red Cliff,
wishing I could harness wild swans and drive.

[J.P.S.]

The Master of Hsiang Plays His Lute

HE plays his cloud-topped lute so well
we hear the Lady-of-the-River.
The god of the stream is moved to dance in
    emptiness.
The traveler of Ch'u can't bear to listen:
a bitter tune to chill both gold and stone.
Pure notes pierce the gloomy dark.
Deep green Wu-t'ung brings sad thoughts on.
White iris there recalls a certain fragrance.
The waters flow between Hsiang's banks.
Mournful winds cross Lake Tung-t'ing.

Song done, and no one to be seen.
On the river, many peaks, all green.

[J.P.S.]

Chiao Jan

(730–799)

Inscribed on the Wall of the Hut by the Lake

If you want to be a mountain-dweller . . .
no need to trek to India to find one.
I've a thousand peaks
to pick from right here on the lake.
Fragrant grasses and white clouds
hold me here.
What holds you there,
world-dweller?

[J.P.S.]

To Be Shown to Monks at a Certain Temple

NOT yet to the shore of non-doing,
it's silly to be sad you're not moored yet.

East Mountain's white clouds say
keep on moving, even
if it's evening,
even if it's fall.

[J.P.S.]

The Creek Out Front

SPRING'S songs already quieting,
the ancient source still bubbles forth.

It's a mistake, my modern friends,
to wound the heart to try
to cross that stream.

[J.P.S.]

*Written at Flower of the Law Temple about
a Monk I Saw Sitting Zazen by the River*

THE road runs into pine sighs—from far off, it's
    even stranger.
Mountain light and colors in the water, tufted,
    raggedy.

On the crag in the middle, in zazen, all alone,
    one monk
sits facing the cassia bough: already old, long ago.

                        [J.P.S.]

WEI YING-WU

(736–830)

On Mount Lang-ya

At Stone Gate there is snow, no trace of travel.
Pine Valley's mists are full of fragrances.

To the crumbs of our meal in the court, cold birds
    come down.
A tattered robe hangs on the tree. The old monk's
    dead.

[J.P.S.]

CHANG CHI
(768–830)

Moored at Maple Bridge

CROWS call in frosty moonlight.
Boat lights glint through maples, keeping me awake.

From far beyond the city, the Han Shan Temple bell
finds my boat at midnight.

[S.H.]

Po Chu-i

(772–846)

After Reading Lao Tzu

"One who speaks does not know; one who knows
    does not speak."
Thus I have been instructed by the Old Master.

If you tell me the Old Master was one who knew,
    I ask,
Why did he write five thousand words to explain it?

[S.H.]

Invitation to Liu the 19th

Clear, fresh Lu-yi sake
warms on my little stove.

This evening sky may bring snow.
Come enjoy a cup with me.

[S.H.]

Liu Tsung-yuan
(773–819)

Snowy River

The birds have vanished
      from a thousand mountains.
On a thousand trails,
      not a single human sign.

A little boat,
      a bamboo hat and cloak—
the old man, alone,
      fishing the snowy river.

[S.H.]

The Old Fisherman

THE old fisherman sleeps under a western cliff.
At dawn, he boils river water and burns bamboo.

When the sun burns off the mist, there's not a soul
    in sight,
only the creak of his oars in green water under
    green hills

where the wide, pale sky and rolling river merge.
Clouds above the cliffs drift wherever they will.

                    [S.H.]

Tu Mu
(803–852)

Spring South of the River

Song of the oriole, a thousand *li,* reds brighten on
    the green.
Streamside village, mountains for walls, wind in
    the tavern banner.

Four hundred eighty temples in the Southern
    Dynasties.
Now how many towers and terraces? The misting
    rain.

[J.P.S.]

Wu Pen (Chia Tao)
(779–843)

Parting with the Monk Ho-lan

Wild monk, come to make a parting with me.
We sit a while on the sand beside the welling
    source.
You'll go a long way on that empty alms bowl,
deep among mountains, treading fallen flowers.
Masterless Ch'an, our own understanding?
When you've got it, there's no place for it but
    a poem.
This parting's nothing fated:
orphan clouds just never settle down.

[J.P.S.]

The Swordsman

Ten long years I've honed this sword:
its frost white blade is yet untried.
Today, like any other gentleman,
it's looking for injustice.

[J.P.S.]

Kuan Hsiu

(832–912)

Bad Government

Sleet and rain, as if the pot were boiling.
Winds whack like the crack of an axe.
An old man, an old old man,
at sunset, crept into my hut.
He sighed. He sighed as if to himself,
"These rulers, so cruel. Why, tell me
why they must steal till we starve,
then slice the skin from our bones?

For a song from some beauty,
they'll go back on sworn words;
for a song from some tart,
they'll tear down our huts;
for a sweet song or two,
they'll slaughter ten thousand like me,
like you. Weep as you will,
let your hair turn white,
let your whole clan go hungry . . .
no good wind will blow,

no gentle breeze
begin again.

Lord Locust Plague and Baron Bandit Bug,
one east, one west, one north, one south.
We're surrounded."

[J.P.S.]

Written in the Mountains

A MOUNTAIN'S a palace
for all things crystalline and pure:
there's not a speck of dust
on a single one of all these flowers.

When we start chanting poems like madmen
it sets all the peaks to dancing.
And once we've put the brush to work
even the sky becomes mere ornament.
For you and me the joy's in the doing
and I'm damned if I care about "talent."

But if, my friend, from time to time
you hear sounds like ghostly laughter,
it's all the great mad poets, dead,
just dropping in to listen.

[J.P.S.]

A Hundred Sorrows

A HUNDRED sorrows under a single sail:
wind and waves, poles of the line of vision,
birds sunk in the mist, and the mountain with
   them.
All the color of the south, still cold next to the skin.

Getting past this place, this autumn of the heart,
one starts to know what hard traveling means.
The evening sun lingers a moment on the sandbar.
I turn my head with one long sigh.

[J.P.S.]

Leaving It to You

SELF evident, truth mistakes no thing.
But my heart's a long way from there
and nothing's very clear.
Yellow gold is almost burned up
by my desire.
White hair grows beside the fire.
Bitter indecision: choose This, or maybe That.
Even the spirit speaks in riddles
and makes it hard to harvest
the essence of a single day.
Catch the wind while you tether shadows.
Faith, or a man who'll stand by his word, is
all there is. There is no disputing.

[J.P.S.]

On Running into the Taoist Master "In Emptiness"

So, say my way differs from yours.
We both have old men's hair and beards.
They say words can kill faith.
I like to arrange spring blossoms in a rough old
    funeral jar.

[J.P.S.]

Seeing a Friend Off Toward Hsi-k'ou

WILD geese go like leaves down the sky.
How should that be easy
for the traveler to hear?

A thousand mountains,
ten thousand streams,
where can we meet again?

Our faces won't last like jade.
Life's more like clouds.

If your way takes you
to the temple
of the Third Patriarch of Zen,

make us all one:
lay an offering by the grave.

[J.P.S.]

Anonymous Sung Dynasty Nun

Searching for spring all day, I never saw it,
straw sandals treading everywhere
among the clouds, along the bank.

Coming home, I laughed, catching
the plum blossom's scent:
spring at each branch tip, already perfect.

[J.P.S./S.H.]

Su Tung-p'o

(1037–1101)

To the Abbot of the Tung-lin Monastery

Sound of the stream is his broad long tongue,
colors of the mountains, the Buddha's body, pure.
In one night they'll sing eighty-four thousand hymns
of praise.
Some other day, will you lecture on them?

[J.P.S]

A Monk at Chi-hsien Temple Asked Me to Name a Hall There

Past the eye: flourishing, withering, lightning
and wind.
For longevity, what's a match for red blossoms?

Where the abbot sits in meditation, he sees the hall,
empty—
seeing what is, seeing what is empty: it *is* what is,
empty.

[J.P.S.]

Written to the Tune of "An Immortal Approaching the River"

WINE at East Bank tonight, sobered up
then started over, getting drunk again.
Got home, a little fuzzy, maybe close to three,
and the houseboy was snoring like thunder.
I knocked at my gate, but nobody answered.
I leaned on my cane and listened to the river.

I hate it!—that even this body's not mine alone . . .
Someday I'll give it all up.
The night moves, the breeze writes
quietly in ripples on the water.
A little boat, leaving here and now,
the rest of my life on the river, on the sea.

[J.P.S.]

Hung-Chih Cheng-chueh
(1090–1157)

Empty Glories

DREAMS, illusions, empty glories—
sixty-seven years.
The white bird disappears in the mist.
Bright autumn waters run straight up to the sky.

[J.P.S.]

Silly Birds

BABY birds leave the nest so easily!
But it's hard as hell
to get the shell
off a wise old tortoise.

[J.P.S.]

Yuan Mei

(1716–1798)

Writing What I've Seen

All things that live
must make a living.
There's nothing got
without some getting.

From fabled beast to feeble bug,
each schemes to make its way.
The Buddha, or the Taoist sage?
Unending in his labor;

morning's herald, the rooster, too—
can he not cock-a-doodle-doo?
I hunger, so I plot to eat;
I'm cold, and would be robed . . .

But great grand schemes will get you grief.
Take what you need, that's all.
A light craft takes the wind
and skims the water lightly.

[J.P.S]

Wandering Late at Kulin Temple

THE single sound of the bell
brings out the whole hall's monks.

Golden glint of the Buddha's face
almost the flash of a lamp.

The bodhisattva Dragon Tree is silent,
the wind has died away . . .

The robes of the monks cast shadows
as the moon begins to rise.

No need to chant to sutras
to make the flowers giggle . . .

As I lean and listen carefully,
even the stones respond.

How can the Buddha, King of Emptiness,
boast of setting the whole world free?

Here, when spring comes,
he hasn't freed even half this pond

from thinking long on love.

[J.P.S.]

Sitting at Night

SITTING at night by the west window,
                    rain everywhere.

Before my eyes the rule of nature's bitter,
                    hard to fathom.

The lamp's gentle gleam becomes a pyre:
from all about, moths come,
                    flight upon flight,
                              into the fire.

                                        [J.P.S.]

On the Road to T'ien-t'ai

WRAPPED, surrounded by ten thousand
    mountains,
cut off, no place to go . . .

Until you're here, there's no way to get here.
Once you're here, there's no way to go.

                                        [J.P.S.]

At the Narrows of the Yung-chia River

For three miles folks' houses
practically straddle the river,
scattered among stones and blossoms,
the householders' hedges.

Their low bramble gates are a little like
the rich man's crimson portals:
you'll have to bow and scrape a bit
if you ever want to enter.

[J.P.S.]

Something to Ridicule

MENCIUS tells us that Confucius, too,
like all the other men of Lu, fought for his share
of what was taken in the hunt: it was
the custom there. To keep oneself in cloisters just
to seek a name for uprightness . . . that
lacks a certain dignity.

But getting learning, too, may be
but putting makeup on.
If one's a whore at heart, he's
sure to act the part.

[J.P.S.]

Last Poem: Goodbye to My Garden

Was I no more than some fairy-being,
strange beast from the *Sutra of Ceylon,*
arisen and set free to play
in Hsiao-ts'ang's summit garden?

Did I know that the garden's guests
of poems and lutes, wine and songs
would also hear the gong of time,
the last dripped drop of the water clock?

My eye roams the towers and pavilions,
and I know these lines are my farewell.
This mountain full of birds will stay,
forever wound and bound in its flowers.

Long ago, an Immortal chose to return
to his home in the form of a crane,
and was almost shot down by a lad with a sling.
If I ever come back to this Paradise,
I'll remember to be careful.

[J.P.S.]

CHING AN

(1851–1912)

Facing Snow and Writing What My Heart Embraces

AT Mount Ssu-ming
in the cold in the snow,
half a lifetime's bitter chanting.
Beard hairs are easy to pluck out
one by one:
a poem's words are hard
to put together.
Pure vanity
to vent the heart and spleen;
words and theories, sometimes, aren't enough.
Loneliness, loneliness
my everyday affair.
The soughing winds
pass on the night bell sound.

[J.P.S.]

Night Sitting

THE hermit doesn't sleep at night:
in love with the blue of the vacant moon
The cool of the breeze
that rustles the trees
rustles him too.

[J.P.S.]

Returning Clouds

MISTY trees hide in crinkled hills' blue green.
The man of the Way's stayed long
at this cottage in the bamboo grove.
White clouds too know the flavor
of this mountain life;
they haven't waited for the vesper bell
to come on home again.

[J.P.S.]

Moored at Maple Bridge

Frost white across the river,
waters reaching toward the sky.
All I'd hoped for's lost
in autumn's darkening.
I cannot sleep, a man
adrift, a thousand miles
alone, among the reed flowers:
but the moonlight fills the boat.

[J.P.S.]

Laughing at Myself (1)

Cold cliff, dead tree,
this knobby-pated me . . .
think there's nothing better than a poem.
I mock myself, writing in the dust, and
damn the man who penned the first word
and steered so many astray.

[J.P.S.]

Laughing at Myself (2)

SLICES of flesh made burnt offerings
to the Buddha.
Just so, I came to know myself,
a ball of mud dissolving in the water.
I had ten fingers. Now, just eight remain.
Did I really think I could become a Buddha
one slice at a time?

[J.P.S.]

PO CHING (SU MAN-SHU)
(1884–1918)

Having Hope, or Holding On

IN this life, how could I hope
to become a Buddha?
Hermit dreams are undependable
and my desires still unconquered.

Many thanks, my friend
for all your kind inquiries,
but I suspect my fate's to be
just a poet-monk.

[J.P.S.]

From Japan

Spring rain on the pagoda roof,
and the *shakuhachi*'s sound.

Will I ever see the Chekiang tidal bore again?
Grass sandals, broken bowl, and no one knows.

Treading on cherry blossoms, I will trudge
across yet one more bridge.

[J.P.S.]

PART TWO

Japanese Poems

Introduction
to the Japanese Poems

BUDDHISM probably entered Japan in the fifth or sixth century via Korea, but the first great Buddhist teacher in Japan was Kūkai (774–835), who denounced Confucianism and Taoism before journeying to the T'ang dynasty capital of Ch'ang-an to study Buddhism in 804. When he returned to Japan a few years later, he established the "True Word" or "True Speech" (*Shingon*) school and became legendary. He was a renowned architect, painter, calligrapher, and sculptor, the author of fifty major essays who is also credited with inventing the Japanese syllabic alphabet (*hiragana*) and who is often called "the father of classical culture." It was Kūkai who planted the roots of Buddhism's place in Japanese arts, crafts, and letters.

There is perhaps the broth of elemental Zen in the poetry of monks like Mansei and Kengei and a few others, but Zen poetry and Zen practice didn't begin to flourish until the late thirteenth and early fourteenth centuries, following the influence of the "Five Mountains" school in Kyoto that produced, among others, such fine poets as Kōhō Kennichi and the indomitable Musō Soseki.

The history of Zen in Japan generally begins with Myōan Eisai (1141–1215) and his elder, Dainichi Nōnin, both of whom brought Chinese Zen practice to Japan, focusing sharply on the teachings of Bodhidarma (Daruma in Japanese). The "Daruma school" grew along with the Rinzai school that carried on the lineage of Chinese master Lin Chi, but neither grew very quickly or established a literary tradition at the beginning. Zen didn't have a major literary teacher until Dōgen Kigen founded the Sōtō school in 1227, following several years of study in China.

Orphaned, Dōgen studied Tendai Buddhism while young and was clearly a remarkable child. It is said he read Chinese poetry at the age of four and knew all the classics by the age of ten. His major collection of essays on Zen practice, *Shōbōgenzō,* runs to ninety-five volumes. He believed that "*Bodhi-mind* [or Buddha-mind] neither existed from the beginning nor arose recently. It is neither one, nor many. It is not the essence of one's self, nor of other selves. It does not arise spontaneously. It is not received from the Buddha or bodhisattvas, nor is it a product of our own making. Rather, it arises only through deep spiritual communion between sentient beings and the Buddha."

He is the Japanese grandmaster advocating *shikantaza,* or "just sitting" in a state of non-meditation, a role almost comparable to Hui Neng's role in Chinese Zen. If Dōgen wasn't often a terrific poet, he was certainly Japan's most influential Zen essayist of the last millennium, and his teachings often turn up in surprising ways in the poetry of Ryōkan and others.

By far the most influential poet in the Japanese Zen tradition wasn't Zen at all, but a Jōdo-shū or "Pure Land" Buddhist before turning to the Shingon ("True Word") school. Saigyō was a famous archer and poet, a monk whose use of *sabi* ("aloneness") in his *waka* (short poems in syllabic lines of 5-7-5-7-7) often opened the eyes of poets and other Zennists to the essential solitariness of serious practice, the solitariness of working toward "enlightenment." Saigyō was also a traveler who made pilgrimages and wrote poems that inspired generations that followed. However much he believed in the "Pure Land" or the "True Word," his poetry holds to the very essence of Zen in its grasp of the "aloneness" of the journey toward realization. He made the tiny hut in the wilderness a grand metaphor as well as a palpable reality of his practice.

While Japanese Zen is a direct product of its Chinese wellspring, it is distinctly Japanese in its second cultural habitat. The Japanese tea ceremony bears little resemblance to the classical Chinese tea ceremony. Outside the temple or the *zendō*, the influence of Zen is seen everywhere in Japanese culture, from corporate gardens to the Noh theatre and musical arts, especially in *shakuhachi* (vertical bamboo flute), and even in modern *butoh* dance. It is in the *tokonoma,* the little alcove given for a scroll and a vase or statue in nearly every home. It lies at the heart of arranging a single flower in a vase, or in pruning a miniature pine in the garden or cultivating bonsai. It is in the straw-fired kilns that produce rough earthen bowls and cups even today. The Zen aesthetic permeates Japanese culture of the last millennium. And yet Zen practice in Japan, as in China, has never really held much appeal for the masses. It is too strict, too severe, allowing for no life after death, no god, no excuses or forgiveness, and no eternal paradise "until all sentient beings become enlightened."

The short Japanese poem is remarkably different than its Chinese counterpart. It relies far more heavily upon refined sensibility than does the Chinese, which is more rooted in juxtaposed imagery. Chinese is written in *kanji,* "characters" that include pictographic elements, each word a single syllable pronounced with a rising, level, falling, or hooked tone. Japanese combines *kanji* that are pronounced differently, but mean the same thing, together with words presented in *kana,* the Japanese phonetic syllabary. Spoken Japanese is fairly level, with a few accented syllables. The standard classical Chinese poem is written in couplets and in lines of either five or seven syllables, in poems of four or eight lines, usually with a set rhyme scheme. The Japanese poem is usually five lines measured syllabically 5-7-5-7-7, with no set rhyme requirement. Most of the great Zen masters and poets of Japan wrote in both languages and styles, often turning to Chinese for their more didactic poems because in Chinese they could more easily include allusions to and paraphrases (*honkadori*) of Zen and poetic and philosophical classics, an important element of their art.

Of course poets like Bashō also used *honkadori* in tanka and haiku. Looking over a great Japanese battleground, Bashō remembers a famous fragment by Tu Fu about how a war had left "the whole country devastated," and "only mountains and rivers remain." Thinking on the nature of war, Bashō wrote:

> Summer grasses:
> all that remains of great soldiers'
> imperial dreams

His poem is a brilliant indictment of the stupidity and cruelty of war, and an eloquently compassionate sigh. His echo of the ancient Chinese reminds the reader of just how little has been learned in a millennium. Tu Fu and Po Chu-i were Bashō's Chinese masters, and Saigyō his literary and spiritual grandfather. In a lifetime of consciously perfecting his practice of both Zen and poetry, indeed of making them one seamless practice, Bashō constantly reexamined his aesthetics, elevating the three-line haiku into an art so clearly superior to anything that preceded or followed him that Japanese poets often remark, "Haiku was born and died with Bashō. Only Issa and Buson approach his standards."

In selecting the poems for this anthology, I have kept monastic teaching poems to a minimum. Most require extensive footnoting for the Western mind to fully understand their content. Zen master Ikkyū Sōjun, for instance, wrote "Joy Amidst Suffering" in the fifteenth century:

> Three cups of sake, and my lips are still dry.
> Old Ts'ao-shan finds solace in poverty and
>   loneliness.
> But rushing into the burning house,
> in one instant we comprehend ten thousand
>   years of pain.

Ts'ao-shan was one of the founders of Sōtō Zen, a school advocating withdrawal from society in pursuit of monastic meditation. The poem refers to a story in which Ts'ao-shan tells a disciple, "You've had three cups of the best sake in China and still you complain that your lips are not wet." The *Lotus Sutra,* the only sutra containing the direct teaching of the Buddha, refers to this life as "a burning house." As scholar James Sanford points out, Ikkyū's poem advocates facing the fire and entering it to "snatch enlightenment from the jaws of death." The instruction is good, but truly coming to understand the poem requires a lot of Zen scholarship as well as practice. There are thousands and thousands of such poems in the Japanese tradition.

I have included a few instructional poems by Saigyō, Dōgen, Ikkyū, Ryōkan, and others, but have for the most part preferred poems that express Zen without talking about it directly, without instructing in practice or scholarship. Poems presented in couplets and quatrains were written in Chinese. Sanford has translated another poem by Ikkyū:

A Natural Way

The Way of the wise is without knowledge.
How long will the pure scholars linger on?
No *Sakyas,* no Maitreyas, in Nature.
In place of ten thousand sutras, one song.

This, I believe, is closer to true Zen. Maitreya is the Buddha of all-encompassing love. The term *Sakyas* refers to the Shakya clan of Shakyamuni, the Buddha. Zen doesn't promise bliss. It doesn't promise a life without suffering of various kinds. And knowing ten thousand sutras is not as good as knowing the song in one's own heart derived from Zen practice.

The "way of poetry" (*kadō*) of Bashō, the "way of letters" of all kinds, is often said to be more an obstacle than an expression of attainment. And yet poetry is useful in a hundred ways and, despite its Confucian insistence upon the "right words in the right order," is one of the primary paths to enlightenment. Dōgen wrote, sounding very much like Lao Tzu:

> Cast away all speech.
> Our words may express it,
> but cannot hold it.
> The way of letters leaves no trace,
> yet the teaching is revealed.

THE PRIEST MANSEI

(CA. 730)

I F pressed to compare
this brief life, I might declare:
It's like the boat
that crossed this morning's harbor,
leaving no mark on the world.

[S.H.]

The Monk Kengei

(CA. 875)

TRUE, I may appear
unkempt like a rotting tree,
jetsam or flotsam,
but on the right occasion
this old heart can still blossom.

[S.H.]

Sōjo Henjō
(816–890)

A FINAL drop of dew
or the first sparkling leaf—
each illustrates
this brief temporal world
in which all things pass through.

[S.H.]

How mysterious!
The lotus remains unstained
by its muddy roots,
delivering shimmering
bright jewels from common dew.

[S.H.]

The Monk Sosei

(D. CA. 909)

WHERE is the dark seed
that grows the forget-you plant?
Searching, now I see
it grows in the frozen heart
of one who has murdered love.

[S.H.]

POETIC justice?
I stand alone with my thoughts
as the crickets cry,
wild pink mountain blossoms
swirling in gathering dusk.

[S.H.]

Ki no Tsurayuki

(D. CA. 945)

Approaching midnight
on a hillside, in springtime,
in a temple hall,
even in my deepest dreams,
the blossoms continue to fall.

[S.H.]

Saigyō
(1118–1190)

I'd like to divide
myself in order to see,
among these mountains,
each and every flower
of every cherry tree.

[S.H.]

Overseeing all
from high in the cherry tree:
even the flowers
grow sad—will they once again
return to greet the spring?

[S.H.]

THOSE who won't discard
all attachments to this world
and accept this life
are doomed to return like gold
to die again and again.

[S.H.]

THIS poor grass-roofed hut
of old brushwood may sound
miserable, but
I very quickly found it
altogether suiting my taste.

[S.H.]

THE titmouse perches
happily among its friends—
a reliable
roost safe among the branches
of the passania tree.

[S.H.]

DEEP in a ravine,
in a tree on the old farm,
a single dove sings
out, searching for a friend,
lonely voice of the evening.

[S.H.]

QUITE the contrary
to what I'd thought, passing clouds
are sometimes simply
the moon's entertainment,
its lovely decoration.

[S.H.]

A Troubled Heart

THE skylark departs,
leaving in the wilderness
a small red lily.
Thus, without friend or attachment,
my heart remains alone.

[S.H.]

DEEP in the mountains,
water splashes down the crags.
If I could stop it,
I'd go in search of wild nuts
that fall this time of year.

[S.H.]

ALONG the trail's edge
beside a sparkling river
in the willow shade,
I lingered to take a nap—
lingered, and I'm still here.

[S.H.]

At the Grave of the Poet Fujiwara Sanekata

(D. 998, EXILED FROM
THE IMPERIAL COURT IN KYOTO)

HE left us nothing
but his own eternal name—
just that final stroke.
One sees only pampas grass
on his poor grave on the moor.

[S.H.]

ON the clear mirror,
just a single speck of dust.
And yet, looking
closely, we see it before
all else—people thinking thus.

[S.H.]

Whom is it calling
in this high mountain village,
that lonely cuckoo?
When I came here, I came
alone, just wanting a life.

[S.H.]

In Tsu country,
that bright Naniwa spring—
was it only a dream?
Only withered reeds remain,
blanketed by cold winds.

[S.H.]

Tock. *Tock.* The spring
water slowly drips down on
mossy rocks—but not
nearly enough for me
to draw for my hermitage.

[S.H.]

In the Rice Fields of Hōzō Temple

With an empty heart
I left society. How
deeply moved I am
when a snipe bursts from the marsh
in the autumn evening

[S.H.]

Touring Kisagata by Boat

In Kisagata,
the flowering cherry trees
vanish under waves—
until an old fisherman
rows out across blossoms.

[S.H.]

This loneliness is
not simply the result
of autumn colors—
even mountain evergreens make
me feel like autumn evening.

[S.H.]

Whatever it is,
I cannot understand it,
although gratitude
stubbornly overcomes me
until I'm reduced to tears.

[S.H.]

My final desire—
that I be allowed to die
under flowering cherries—
on the fifteenth evening
of the second month.

[S.H.]

Before the Buddha
lay sweet cherry blossom
garlands if you should
wish to ease my entry
into the world to come.

[S.H.]

Fujiwara no Ietaka

(1158–1237)

Everything must end.
Thus the day tries to begin
with the morning bell.
But the long night remains,
empty moon still in the sky.

[S.H.]

THE PRIEST JAKUREN

(1139–1202)

> CALL it loneliness,
> that deep, beautiful color
> no one can describe:
> over these dark mountains,
> the gathering autumn dusk.

[S.H.]

FUJIWARA NO TEIKA

(1162–1241)

> You who fail to think
> on the transience of things,
> listen: do you hear,
> in that far mountain village,
> a duck cries on the frozen pond?

[S.H.]

Asukai Masatsune

(1170–1221)

I walked among stones
through mountains of mountains,
paying no mind
until the flower-trail behind
turned into drifting white clouds.

[S.H.]

DŌGEN KIGEN

(1200–1253)

LONGER than the tails
of wandering mountain pheasants
on foot-tiring hills,
the long night lies before me,
though it too leads into dawn.

[S.H.]

EVEN without hearts
and minds, plants wither
with the passing days.
Seeing just how this is so,
we feel a little ashamed.

[S.H.]

CAST away all speech.
Our words may express it,
but cannot hold it.
The way of letters leaves no trace,
yet the teaching is revealed.

[S.H.]

Kōhō Kennichi

(1241–1316)

So you must persist
in asking where my heart goes
all the long, cold night.
Like following trails left by birds
who vanished with yesterday's sky.

[S.H.]

Here in a thatched hut
hidden among mountain peaks,
with barely room for one,
I'm suddenly invaded
by wandering white clouds.

[S.H.]

EMPEROR FUSHIMA

(1265–1317)

Only now I know
that power—greater than storms—
a heart-rending awe
silencing all the pines
at nightfall on the mountain.

[S.H.]

Empress Eifuku Mon-in
(1271–1342)

It's on-rushing time,
seasons blown by passing winds
that trouble us so.
In the heart of the flower
there is no need to leave this world.

[S.H.]

MUSŌ SOSEKI
(1275–1351)

"SATORI" noted,
the mind, like quicksilver, goes,
falsely "enlightened,"
down those old wrongheaded roads,
each more wrong than one before.

[S.H.]

IF only people
would not come to visit me
in lonely mountains
where I have built my retreat
from the world's many trials.

[S.H.]

Ikkyū Sōjun

(1394–1481)

Essentially,
all previous lives and selves
are gone from nature—
without destination,
without place, without value.

[S.H.]

At a way station,
returning from Drizzly Road
to Always Dry Road:
if it should rain, it will rain;
if the wind should blow, it blows.

[S.H.]

WITHOUT beginning,
utterly without end,
the mind is born
to struggles and distresses,
and dies—and that is emptiness.

[S.H.]

LIKE vanishing dew,
a passing apparition
or the sudden flash
of lightning—already gone—
thus should one regard one's self.

[S.H.]

THE moon is a house
in which the mind is master.
Look very closely:
only impermanence lasts.
This floating world, too, will pass.

[S.H.]

AND what is mind
and how is it recognized?
It is clearly drawn
in sumi ink, the sound
of breezes drifting through pine.

[S.H.]

A Warning Against Dozing

Passing an upturned carriage,
the driver's suddenly awakened.
Surrendering to sleep invites disaster.

Neither drunk nor sober,
I wander out late:

A crow calls. The moon
sinks into the tolling of the midnight bell.

[S.H.]

Shakyamuni's Austerities

Six years of piercing cold and hunger!
Shakyamuni's way demands austerity.

Anyone who thinks buddhahood is easy
is just a rice bag in a monk's robe.

[S.H.]

Song of the Dream Garden

Pillowed on your thighs in a dream garden,
little flower with its perfumed stamen,

singing, sipping from the stream of you—
Sunset. Moonlight. Our song continues.

[S.H.]

Face-to-Face with My Lover on Daitō's Anniversary

MONKS recite the sutras in honor of the founder,
their many voices cacophonous in my ear.

Afterward, making love, our intimate whispers
mock the empty formal discipline of others.

[S.H.]

My Hand Is Lady Mori's Hand

MY hand is Lady Mori's hand
and knows her mastery of love.

When I am weak, she resurrects my jeweled stem.
The monks I train are happy then.

[S.H.]

Elegy

WE first lay down among flowers
ten years ago and found a timeless rapture.

Sadly, I remember being pillowed by her lap,
all-night love, all eternity in our vows.

[S.H.]

Sōgi

(1421–1502)

Everyone's journey
through this world is the same,
so I won't complain.
Here on the plains of Nasu,
I place my trust in the dew.

[S.H.]

To each thing, its own
true deepest inner nature:
water does not think
of itself as consort
of the bright moonlight it hosts.

[S.H.]

Sōin

(1604–1682)

Settling, white dew
does not discriminate,
each drop its home

[S.H.]

Anonymous

(CA. 1700)

CHANTING Buddha's name
is the deepest pleasure
of one's old age

[S.H.]

To learn how to die,
watch cherry blossoms, observe
chrysanthemums

[S.H.]

Matsuo Bashō

(1644–1694)

Selections from
Narrow Road to the Interior

Very early on the twenty-seventh morning of third moon, under a predawn haze, transparent moon still visible, Mount Fuji just a shadow, I set out under the cherry blossoms of Ueno and Yanaka. When would I see them again? A few old friends had gathered in the night and followed along far enough to see me off from the boat. Getting off at Senju, I felt three thousand miles rushing through my heart, the whole world only a dream. I saw it through farewell tears.

> Spring passes
> and the birds cry out—tears
> in the eyes of fishes

With these first words from my brush, I started. Those who remain behind watch the shadow of a traveler's back disappear.

∾

At Ashino, the willow Saigyō praised, "beside the clear stream," still grows along a path in fields of rice. A local official had offered to lead the way, and I had often wondered whether and where it remained. And now, today, that same willow:

> Rice-planting done, they
> depart—before I emerge
> from willow shade

~

We spent several days in Sukagawa with the poet Tokyu, who asked about the Shirakawa Barrier. "With mind and body sorely tested," I answered, "busy with other poets' lines, engaged in splendid scenery, it's hardly surprising I didn't write much":

> Culture's beginnings:
> from the heart of the country
> rice-planting songs

~

Here three generations of the Fujiwara clan passed as though in a dream. The great outer gates lay in ruins. Where Hidehira's manor stood, rice fields grew. Only Mount Kinkei remained. I climbed the hill where Yoshitsune died; I saw the Kitakami, a broad stream flowing down through the Nambu Plain, the Koromo River circling Izumi Castle below the hill before joining the Kitakami. The ancient ruins of Yasuhira—from the end of the Golden Era— lie out beyond the Koromo Barrier where they stood guard against the Ainu people. The faithful elite remained bound to the castle, for all their valor, reduced to ordinary grass. Tu Fu wrote:

> The whole country devastated
> only mountains and rivers remain.
> In springtime, at the ruined castle,
> the grass is always green.

We sat a while, our hats for a seat, seeing it all through tears.

> Summer grasses:
> all that remains of great soldiers'
> imperial dreams

The road through the Nambu Plain visible in the distance, we stayed the night in Iwate, then trudged on past Cape Oguro and Mizu Island, both along the river. Beyond Narugo Hot Springs, we crossed Shitomae Barrier and entered Dewa province. Almost no one comes this way, and the barrier guards were suspicious, slow, and thorough. Delayed, we climbed a steep mountain in falling dark, and took refuge in a guardshack. A heavy storm pounded the shack with wind and rain for three miserable days.

Eaten alive by
lice and fleas—now the horse
beside my pillow pees

~

In Yamagata province, the ancient temple founded by
Jikaku Daishi in 860, Ryūshaku Temple is stone quiet,
perfectly tidy. Everyone told us to see it. It meant a few
miles extra, doubling back toward Obanazawa to find
shelter. Monks at the foot of the mountain offered
rooms, then we climbed the ridge to the temple,
scrambling up through ancient gnarled pine and oak,
gray smooth stones and moss. The temple doors, built
on rocks, were bolted. I crawled among boulders to
make my bows at shrines. The silence was profound. I
sat, feeling my heart begin to open.

Lonely stillness—
a single cicada's cry
sinking into stone

~

At the Echizen Province border, at an inlet town
called Yoshizaki, I hired a boat and sailed for the fa-
mous pines of Shiogoshi. Saigyō wrote:

All the long night
salt-winds drive
storm-tossed waves

and moonlight drips
through Shiogoshi pines.

This one poem says enough. To add another would be like adding a sixth finger to a hand.

Selections from TRAVELOGUE OF WEATHER-BEATEN BONES

I LEFT MY RUNDOWN hut beside the river during the eighth month of 1684, placing my trust in my walking stick and in the words of the Chinese sage who said, "I pack no provisions for my long journey—entering emptiness under the midnight moon." The voice of the wind was oddly cold.

> Weather-beaten bones,
> I'll leave your heart exposed
> to cold, piercing winds

On the bank of the Fuji River, we came upon an abandoned child, about age two, its sobs stirring our pity. The child's parents must have been crushed by the waves of this floating world to have left him here beside the rushing river to pass like dew. I thought the harsh autumn winds would surely scatter the bush clover blossoms in the night or wither them—and him—in the frosty dew of dawn. I left him what food I could.

> Hearing the monkey's cries—
> what of the child abandoned
> to the autumn wind?

I arrived at my old village early in the ninth month. All the grass beside North Hall had been consumed by frost. Nothing was the same. My brothers had grown gray at the temples, wrinkled around their eyes. All we could say was, "How good to be alive, to meet again!"

My older brother opened a small amulet, saying, "Bow to your mother's white hair. This is like the famous jeweled box of Urashima Tarō—your own eyebrows have already turned gray!"

I wrote this after we had all shed our tears:

> If I took it in hand,
> it would melt in my hot tears—
> heavy autumn frost

I wandered on alone into the mountainous heart of the Yoshino region where great white clouds piled high among mountain tops and rain veiled the valleys. A few woodcutters' cabins dotted the hills. The sound of axes ringing on the western slope were echoed by eastern mountains, only to be answered by temple bells that reached my very core.

Of all the men who have entered these mountains to live the reclusive life, most found solace in ancient poetry, so it might be appropriate to compare this countryside to Mount Lu, where many famous Chinese poets sought seclusion.

I found a night's lodging at a temple hostel:

> At her fulling block
> she makes beautiful music,
> the good temple wife

Saigyō's thatched roof hut once stood a few hundred yards from the inner temple, and could be reached only by way of a narrow woodsman's trail. It looked across a deep, breathtaking valley. The "trickling clear water" made famous by the poet could still be heard.

> With clear melting dew,
> I'd try to wash away the dust
> of this floating world

If Po-i had been Japanese, he'd no doubt have washed his mouth here. If Hsu Yu knew of it, he'd have washed out his ears here.

Autumn sunset had begun while I was still on the mountain trail, so I decided to forego other famous sites, choosing to visit the tomb of Emperor Go Daigo (1288–1339):

At the royal tomb—
and what does it remember,
this "remembrance grass"?

Selections from THE KNAPSACK NOTEBOOK

IT WAS MID-AUTUMN under threatening skies when I made up my mind to begin a journey. Windblown leaves reminded me of all the uncertainties a wanderer faces.

> A wanderer,
> let that be my name—
> the first winter rain

From the earliest times, the art of the travel journal has been appreciated by readers. The great Ki no Tsurayuki wrote the famous *Tosa Journal*, and Kamo no Chomei recorded life in a ten-foot square hut. The nun Abutsu perfected the genre. All the rest merely imitate these masters. My brush, lacking both wisdom and inspiration, strives vainly to be their equal.

How easy it is to observe that a morning began with rain only to become sunny in the afternoon; that a pine tree stood at a particular place, or to note the name of a river bend. This is what people write in their journals. Nothing's worth noting that is not seen with fresh eyes. You will find in my notebook random observations from along the road, experiences and images that linger in heart and mind—a secluded house in the mountains, a lonely inn on a moor.

I write in my notebook with the intention of stimulating good conversation, hoping that it will also be of use to some fellow traveler. But perhaps my notes are mere drunken chatter, the incoherent babbling of a dreamer. If so, read them as such.

They say the ancient poet Sōgi nearly starved to death in the high village of Hinaga. I hired a horse to help me over Walking-Stick Pass. Unfamiliar with horses and tack, both saddle and rider took a tumble.

> If I'd walked Walking-
> Stick Pass, I'd not have fallen
> from my horse

As my worn-out feet dragged me along, I was reminded of Saigyō and how much he suffered along the banks of Tenryū River. When I hired a horse, I remembered a famous priest who was humiliated when his horse threw him into a moat.

I was moved nonetheless by the beauty of the natural world, rarely seen mountain vistas and coastlines. I visited the temporary hermitages of ancient sages. Even better, I met people who had given over their whole lives to the search for truth in art. With no real home of my own, I wasn't interested in accumulating treasures. And since I traveled empty-handed, I didn't worry much about robbers.

I walked at a leisurely pace, preferring my walk even to riding a palanquin, eating my fill of coarse vegetables while refusing meat. My way turned on a whim since I had no set route to follow. My only concerns were whether I'd find suitable shelter for the night or how well straw sandals fit my feet. Each twist in the road brought new sights, each dawn renewed my inspiration. Wherever I met another person with even the least appreciation for artistic excellence, I was overcome with joy. Even those I'd expected to be stubbornly old-fashioned often proved to be good companions. People often say that the greatest pleasures of traveling are finding a sage hidden behind weeds or treasures hidden in trash, gold among discarded pottery. Whenever I encountered someone of genius, I wrote about it in order to tell my friends.

It was early summer when I walked along Suma Beach, thin clouds overhead, the moon particularly beautiful as nights grew shorter. The mountains were dark with new growth. Just as I thought it must be time to hear the first cuckoo, the eastern horizon began to glow and the hills around Ueno grew red and brown with wheat fields except where fishermen's huts dotted fields of white poppies.

> At dawn, the brown faces
> of fishermen emerge from
> fields of white poppies

Selected Haiku

On New Year's Day,
each thought a loneliness as
autumn dusk descends

[S.H.]

New Year's first snow—ah—
just barely enough to tilt
the daffodil

[S.H.]

Between our two lives
there is also the life of
the cherry blossom

[S.H.]

Under full blossom—
a spirited monk and
a flirtatious wife

[S.H.]

Within the skylark's song—
the distinct rhythm of
the pheasant's cry

[S.H.]

Kannon's tiled temple
roof floats far away in clouds
of cherry blossoms

[S.H.]

How very noble!
One who finds no satori
in the lightning flash

[S.H.]

UNLOADING its freight,
spilling new rainwater,
the camellia bends

[S.H.]

ON a bare branch,
a solitary crow—
autumn evening

[S.H.]

THE housecat's lover
visits her frequently
through the burnt-out oven

[S.H.]

AT the ancient pond
a frog plunges into
the sound of water

[S.H.]

For those who proclaim
they've grown weary of children,
there are no flowers

[S.H.]

Now I see her face,
the old woman, abandoned,
the moon her only companion

[S.H.]

Nothing in the cry
of cicadas suggests they
are about to die

[S.H.]

Delight, then sorrow
afterward—aboard the
cormorant fishing boat

[S.H.]

Now a cuckoo's song
carries the haiku master
right out of this world

[S.H.]

A trapped octopus—
one night of dreaming
with the summer moon

[S.H.]

The bee emerging
from deep within the peony
departs reluctantly

[S.H.]

I slept at a temple—
and now with such seriousness
I watch the moon

[S.H.]

UNDER bright moonlight,
the Four Gates and the Four Sects
are only one!

[S.H.]

DRINKING sake
brings on insomnia—
it snowed all night

[S.H.]

A WHITE chrysanthemum—
and to meet the viewer's eye,
not a mote of dust.

[S.H.]

EVEN the whitefish
opens black eyes to the law
of Buddha's net

[S.H.]

On a Portrait of Hotei, God of Good Fortune

How much I desire!
Inside my little satchel,
the moon, and flowers

[S.H.]

TREMBLE, oh my grave—
in time my cries will be
only this autumn wind

[S.H.]

KIKAKU
(1661–1707)

O GREAT Buddha,
your lap must be filling with
these flowers of snow

[S.H.]

IN the Emperor's bed,
the smell of burnt mosquitoes,
and erotic whispers

[S.H.]

ONITSURA
(1660–1738)

To finally know
the plum, use the whole heart too,
and your own nose

[S.H.]

THE leaping trout sees
far below, a few white clouds
as they flow

[S.H.]

BUSON
(1715–1783)

PRIESTLY poverty—
he carves a wooden Buddha
through a long cold night

[S.H.]

CLINGING to the bell,
he dozes so peacefully,
this new butterfly

[S.H.]

THE camellia tips,
the remains of last night's rain
splashing out

[S.H.]

WITH no underrobes,
bare butt suddenly exposed—
a gust of spring wind

[S.H.]

SWEET springtime showers,
and no words can express
how sad it all is

[S.H.]

HEAD pillowed on arm,
such affection for myself!
and this smoky moon

[S.H.]

THE late evening crow
of deep autumn longing
suddenly cries out

[S.H.]

IN a bitter wind
a solitary monk bends
to words cut in stone

[S.H.]

THIS cold winter night,
that old wooden-head Buddha
would make a nice fire

[S.H.]

UTTER aloneness—
another great pleasure
in autumn twilight

[S.H.]

NOBLY, the great priest
deposits his daily stool
in bleak winter fields

[S.H.]

RYŌKAN
(1758–1831)

Chinese Style Poems

I KNOW a gentleman poet
who writes in the high old way—

master of form from Han and Wei
or new-style modeled on the T'ang.

With elegant strokes, he quietly composes,
deftly adding images to startle.

But he hasn't learned to speak from the heart:
all wasted! Though he writes all night long.

[S.H.]

WHO says my poems are poems?
They aren't poems at all.

Only when you understand my poems aren't poems
can we talk poetry.

[S.H.]

IN my hut, I keep *Han Shan's Poems*.
They're better than any sutra.

I copy out his poems and pin them up
and recite them again and again.

[S.H.]

No bird above these wild hills.
Garden leaves fall one by one.

Desolate autumn winds.
A man alone in thin black robes.

[S.H.]

(Poem in Four Characters)

ABOVE heaven
big winds

[S.H.]

NOTHING satisfies some appetites,
but wild plants ease my hunger.

Free of untoward desires,
all things bring me pleasure.

Tattered robes warm frozen bones.
I wander with deer for companions.

I sing to myself like a crazy man
and children sing along.

[S.H.]

I NEVER longed for the wilder side of life.
Rivers and mountains were my friends.

Clouds consumed my shadow where I roamed,
and birds pass high above my resting place.

Straw sandals in snowy villages,
a walking stick in spring,

I sought a timeless truth: the flowers' glory
is just another form of dust.

[S.H.]

You stop to point at the moon in the sky,
but the finger's blind unless the moon is shining.

One moon, one careless finger pointing—
are these two things or one?

The question is a pointer guiding
a novice from ignorance thick as fog.

Look deeper. The mystery calls and calls:
No moon, no finger—nothing there at all.

[S.H.]

As a boy, I studied literature
but failed to become a scholar.

I sat for years in zazen,
but failed my Dharma Master.

Now I inhabit a hut
inside a Shinto shrine:

half common custodian,
half devotee of the Buddha.

[S.H.]

Sixty years a poor recluse alone
in a hut near a cliffside shrine.

Night rains fall and carve the cliff.
On my sill, my candle sputters in the wind.

[S.H.]

The winds have died, but flowers go on falling;
birds call, but silence penetrates each song.

The Mystery! Unknowable, unlearnable.
The virtue of Kannon.

[S.H.]

Japanese Poems

THE leaves begin to
fall—and lie where they fall,
in the garden grass

[S.H.]

WAS it all a dream—
I mean those old bygone days—
were they what they seemed?
All night long I lie awake
listening to autumn rain.

[S.H.]

WHAT might I leave you
as my lasting legacy—
flowers in springtime,
the cuckoo singing all summer,
the yellow leaves of autumn.

[S.H.]

To kindle a fire,
the autumn winds have piled
a few dead leaves

[S.H.]

RYŌKAN, if
anyone should ask, had
these last words for the world:
Namu Amida Butsu—
and offered nothing more.

[S.H.]

KOBAYASHI ISSA

(1763–1827)

Selections from THE SPRING OF MY LIFE

STILL CLOTHED IN THE DUST of this suffering world, I celebrate the first day in my own way. And yet I am like the priest, for I too shun trite popular seasonal congratulations. The commonplace "crane" and "tortoise" echo like empty words, like the actors who come begging on New Year's Eve with empty wishes for prosperity. The customary New Year pine will not stand beside my door. I won't even sweep my dusty house, living as I do in a tiny hermitage constantly threatening to collapse under harsh north winds. I leave it all to the Buddha, as in the ancient story.

The way ahead may be dangerous, steep as snowy trails winding through high mountains. Nevertheless I welcome the New Year just as I am.

> New Year greeting-time:
> I feel about average
> welcoming my spring

In cherry blossom
shadows, no one, really, is
a stranger now

Written on Buddha's Death Day
[March 15, 1819]

Aloof and silent
like the Buddha, I lie still—
still troubled by flowers

Even as he sleeps,
Buddha smilingly accepts
flowers and money

During meditation:

He glares back at me
with an ugly, surly face,
this old pond frog

Several people told me a story about some folks who
heard heavenly music at two in the morning on New
Year's Day. Furthermore, they all said, these people
have heard it again every eighth day since. They de-

scribed exactly when and where each hearing occurred.

Some people laughed it off as the trickeries of the wind, but I was reluctant to either accept or dismiss the story without evidence. Heaven and earth are home to many mysteries. We all know the stories of dancing girls who pour the morning dew from high above. Perhaps the spirits who observe from the corridors of the heavens, seeing a peaceful world, called for music to rejoice. And perhaps we who failed to hear it were deafened by our own suffering.

I invited a few friends to visit my hermitage the morning of March 19th, and we spent the whole night listening. By the time first light broke in the east, we'd heard nothing. Then, suddenly, we heard singing from the plum tree outside a window.

Just a bush warbler
to sing morning *Lotus Sutra*
to this suffering world

Summer's first melon
lies firmly hugged to the breast
of a sleeping child

Buzzing noisily
by my ear, the mosquito
must know I'm old

I've had this in mind for a long time, trying to find a
way to say it:

> Even the flies
> in the village of my birth
> draw blood with each bite

> When I bowed before
> the Buddha, hungry mosquitoes
> swarmed from his shadow

> My home is so poor
> even the resident flies
> keep their family small

> Lying in hammocks,
> we speak so solemnly of
> distant thunder, distant rain

Toshiyori wrote:

> Lured by the branches
> set out to trap them, fish thrash
> helplessly about.
> Likewise people are enticed
> by the lures of ignorance.

Kōsetsu wrote:

> I'd love to slap that
> fly on the beautiful face
> of my young stepchild

It is often said that the greatest pleasures result in the greatest misery. But why is it that my little child, who's had no chance to savor even half the world's pleasures—who should be green as new needles on the eternal pine—why should she be found on her deathbed, puffy with blisters raised by the despicable god of smallpox? How can I, her father, stand by and watch her fade away each day like a perfect flower suddenly ravaged by rain and mud?

Two or three days later, her blisters dried to hard scabs and fell off like dirt softened by melting snow. Encouraged, we made a tiny boat of straw and poured hot sake over it with a prayer and sent it floating downriver in hopes of placating the god of the pox. But our hope and efforts were useless and she grew weaker day by day. Finally, at midsummer, as the morning glory flowers were closing, her eyes closed forever.

Her mother clutched her cold body and wailed. I knew her heartbreak but also knew that tears were useless, that water under the bridge never returns, that scattered flowers are gone forever. And yet nothing I could do would cut the bonds of human love.

> This world of dew
> is only the world of dew—
> and yet . . . and yet . . .

~

In the classic collection of Zen koans, *Mumonkan,* it is written:

> He comes without lifting a foot;
> he teaches without moving his tongue.
> However you lead the way, remember:
> There is always one you follow.

~

In a temple storehouse:

> Smiling serenely,
> the Buddha gently points to
> a little stinkworm

~

Visiting my daughter's grave on July 25th, one month after her death:

> The red flower
> you always wanted to pick—
> now this autumn wind

Pretending wisdom,
a man tells a woman all
about the eclipse
Backwards, ass over
teakettle, the small boy held
fast to his radish

Selected Haiku

ALL around my house,
pond frogs, from the beginning,
sang about old age

[S.H.]

AT the flowerpot,
the butterfly listens:
true Buddha dharma

[S.H.]

BUDDHA beside a field,
and blooming from his nose,
a long icicle

[S.H.]

THE winter fly
I caught and finally freed
the cat quickly ate

[S.H.]

THIS suffering world:
the flowers will blossom, but
even at that . . .

[S.H.]

HERE in Shinano
are famous moons, and buddhas,
and our good noodles

[S.H.]

THE distant mountains
are reflected in the eye
of the dragonfly

[S.H.]

THE old dog listens
intently, as if to the
worksongs of the worms

[S.H.]

DON'T kill that poor fly!
He cowers, wringing
his hands for mercy

[S.H.]

FROM the Great Buddha's
great nose, a swallow comes
gliding out

[S.H.]

A WORLD of dew,
and within every dewdrop
a world of struggle

[S.H.]

IN the midst of this world
we stroll along the roof of hell
gawking at flowers

[S.H.]

A WORLD of trials,
and if the cherry blossoms,
it simply blossoms

[S.H.]

AFTER a long nap,
the cat yawns, rises, and goes out
looking for love

[S.H.]

THE field worker
wipes his snotty fingers
on the plum blossom

[S.H.]

LONELINESS already
planted with each seed in
morning glory beds

[S.H.]

IN early spring rain
the ducks that were not eaten
are quacking happy

[S.H.]

FROM birthing's washbowl
to the washbowl of the dead –
blathering nonsense!

[S.H.]

NOTES ON THE POETS

Chinese Poets

Poets are listed here in order of appearance.

Lao Tzu (4th century BCE) is "The Old Master," the legendary grandfather of Taoism. His masterpiece, *Tao Te Ching*, or "Classic of the Way and Its Virtue," is often referred to as "The Five Thousand Word Classic."

T'ao Ch'ien (365–427), also called T'ao Yuan-ming, was born in Kiangsi province and spent his life as a sometimes impoverished farmer. His poetry reflects the complete fusion of Confucian conviction and Taoist spirituality. Although his poetry remained almost unknown during his lifetime, he came to be venerated as "the grandfather of poetry" by the generations that followed.

Hsieh Ling-yun (385–433), who became the Duke of K'ang-lo, was one of the most influential poets in Chinese history, bringing Buddhist practice and insight to classical "nature poetry," a term he would have disliked.

HUI YUNG (4th–5th century) was one of the early monk-poet translators who introduced Taoist terminology into translations of the sutras. He emphasized meditation and encouraged the lay community to take up sitting practice and to socialize with literate monks.

WANG FAN-CHIH (590–660) is a mystery. There are two extant manuscripts attributed to "Wang, Buddhist Devotee," which is what his name means. One of them was clearly composed by a witty Zen teacher, and these poems were extremely popular and influential during the T'ang dynasty.

HSUAN CHUEH (665–713) was a student of T'ien-t'ai Buddhism, then of Hui Neng, whom he sought out in the Pao-lin Monastery. He is said to have mastered "walking, standing, sitting and lying meditation," and his long *Cheng Tao Ko,* from which these poems are taken, is studied as scripture.

HAN SHAN (8th century) was a Zen tramp who scribbled poems on his cave wall and on rocks and trees around temples, shrines, and monasteries in the T'ien-t'ai Mountain region of east central China. While it is not as rough as Wang Fan-chih's poetry, the polite upper class found Han Shan's straightforward style (*majen, tajen,* "cursing and hitting people") about to be as "refreshing" as being whacked by the master's stick in the meditation hall. His poetry was—and is—countercultural. It is his direct, unpolished manner that has endeared him to centuries of readers.

SHIH TE (ca. 730). "The Shih Te Poems" are a collection of the earliest poems written by a variety of poets, some better than others, in the style of Han Shan. In the early T'ang, most imitators preferred to write under the pseudonym Shih Te, "The Foundling." By the Sung dynasty, all kinds of poets wrote openly "in the manner of Han Shan."

MENG HAO-JAN (689–740) was born in Hupeh province and spent his first forty years on remote Lumen Shan, "Deer Gate Mountain," after failing to pass examination for holding office. His poems are often compared with those of his friends, Wang Wei and Wang Ch'ang-ling. All three sought the contemplative qualities of rural life in simple, direct syntax. He is a strong link in the long chain of Zen poets being at one with nature, and was greatly admired by Li Po and Tu Fu.

WANG CH'ANG-LING (689–756) was, during his lifetime, considered the "supreme poet of the empire," and enjoyed far greater popularity than Li Po or other well well-known poets of his time. His quatrains in seven character lines were particularly famous. After his death during the An Lu-shan Rebellion, he was mourned by all the poets and by many eminent Taoist and Buddhist clerics.

LI PO (701–761) is China's most famous poet. Imprisoned as a traitor, pardoned, exiled, celebrated, granted amnesty, he lived on the edge, a panhandler, epic drinker, and self-promoter par excellence. He claimed never to have revised a line in his poems, and practiced *zazen.* Legend says he drowned in exile, trying to embrace the reflection of the moon in a river.

WANG WEI (701–761) was perhaps China's first great publicly celebrated Buddhist poet. Imprisoned at the Bodhi Temple in the capital city, Chang-an, during the An Lu-shan Rebellion, he later excelled as a courtier and was admired as a poet, landscape painter, and musician. His "Wang River Poems" are among the masterpieces of his age. He died while serving in the State Department.

CH'ANG CHIEN (708–765?) passed the coveted civil service examinations, then rejected the opportunity to accept a comfortable position in the Confucian bureaucracy, choosing instead a reclusive life. He wrote about the frontier regions as well as along Buddhist and Taoist themes.

Liu Ch'ang-ch'ing (ca. 710–785?) passed the civil service examinations in 733 and held several middle-level posts before fleeing central China during the An Lu-shan Rebellion. Only later did he emerge as one of the best poets of the generation following Tu Fu, Wang Wei, and Li Po.

Tu Fu (712–770), the "Poetry Sage" (*shih sheng*), was born to a family fallen from nobility. Failing his civil service examinations, he spent years as a wanderer, living in poverty, but a model of Confucian conduct. He drew inspiration from the suffering he observed in his travels, much of it the result of ruthless inscription and unfair taxation. His poetry was largely unacknowledged in his lifetime, and only 1,554 of his ten thousand poems survive.

Ch'ien Ch'i (722–780?) was regarded as among the best of the post–An Lu-shan Rebellion poets, and was favorably compared to Wang Wei.

Chiao Jan (730–799), was a distant relative of Hsieh Ling-yun, and became one of the first recognized Ch'an-master poets and was a noted literary critic. He gave up writing poetry when he felt that his attachment to it stood between himself and enlightenment.

Wei Ying-wu (736–830) served in the Imperial

Guard before becoming a provincial official celebrated for his generous patronage of poets. His poems reflect the influence of T'ao Ch'ien and Wang Wei.

CHANG CHI (768–830) spent a lifetime in poverty, but, with the literary patronage of Han Yu and others, wrote many poems in the "folk song style," denouncing social injustice, as well as elegies and meditative poems.

PO CHU-I (772–846) is, along with Tu Fu, Wang Wei, and Li Po, among the best known of all Chinese poets in the West. He was courageous in criticizing social injustice and was revered for his loyalty to friends. Like many of his contemporaries, he spent years in exile, but eventually achieved a high position in the court and adopted the Buddhist name "Lay Buddhist of Fragrant Mountain." He wrote about ten thousand poems.

LIU TSUNG-YUAN (773–819) was born and lived in the capital city of Ch'ang-an, but for fifteen years he spent in exile in the south.

TU MU (803–852) claimed to have earned a reputation for hanging around courtesans' quarters, but was in fact a popular poet who was also governor of four districts. He lived happily in Hangchow at the mouth of the Yangtze River, where he was called "Little Tu" to distinguish him from Tu Fu.

Wu Pen (Chia Tao) (779–843) was raised in a monastery and began adult life as a Ch'an monk with a Buddhist name. He was "discovered" by the poet and Confucian official Han Yu, reportedly arguing with himself over a verb in a poem. Under Han Yu's patronage, as Chia Tao, he left monastic life to become a government official, as Ch'an advocates, using "efficacious means" for working for the salvation of all sentient beings. He continued to be a great Zen poet.

Kuan Hsiu (832–912) was regarded by his contemporaries as the greatest poet of the last years of the T'ang dynasty. An innovative portrait painter as well, he was a master technician in verse forms ranging from the four-character lines of his "Poetry Classic" to the varying measures of the newly popular *tz'u* poetry in which new lyrics were written to older tunes.

Anonymous Sung Dynasty Nun: There are very few poems by women in the Ch'an collections, and most are, like this one, anonymous.

Su Tung-p'o (1037–1101), also called Su Shih, was deeply schooled in Taoism before becoming a devoted student of Zen. He suffered several banishments, but was renowned as a compassionate and benevolent administrator in the provinces. He is generally considered to be the greatest poet of the Sung dynasty.

HUNG-CHIH CHENG-CHUEH (1090–1157) was able to recite the Five Confucian Classics by memory before he entered a monastery at age eleven, where he led an active religious life.

YUAN MEI (1716–1798) was probably the most widely read poet of the Ch'ing dynasty. His writing clearly shows how deeply the Zen worldview had penetrated Chinese society by the time of the final traditional dynasty. He was a good Confucian official until he resigned over a conflict that threatened to compromise his principles. He practiced *zazen*, made pilgrimages to Buddhists sites, and wrote poetry in praise of the world as it is and as it may become.

CHING AN (1851–1912) was said to have made up poems even before he learned to write. Monastically educated, he mocked the "worldly attachment" that poetry seemed, paradoxically, to represent. Late in life he was unsuccessful in serving the monasteries of east central China in negotiations with the new "republic" in Peking as he struggled to preserve the great Buddhist heritage they represented.

PO CHING (SU MAN-SHU) (1884–1918), probably better known as Su Man-shu, was the son of a Cantonese merchant and a Japanese woman. He traveled widely, including teaching in Indonesia, before settling back in China. He bought—or perhaps stole—his monk's license. Nevertheless, as a famous secular romantic poet, he promoted Buddhism and began the first modern Sanskrit grammar in Chinese.

Japanese Poets

THE PRIEST MANSEI (ca. 730), also called Kasamaro, was a friend and collaborator of the great poet Otomo no Yakamochi, and is included in the first Imperial anthology, the *Man'yōshū*.

THE MONK KENGEI (ca. 875–900) was a priest from Shirogami in Yamato province.

SŌJO HENJŌ (816-890) is one of the "six geniuses of poetry" (*rokkasen*). Despite being the grandson of an emperor, he left court life to become a Buddhist "high priest" (*sōjō*). He is rumored to have carried on an intense love affair with Ono no Komachi, who is generally thought to be the greatest female poet of ancient Japan.

THE MONK SOSEI (d. ca. 909) was a *renga* (linked verse) master whose travel journals were an inspiration and model for Bashō. His name is linked forever with Kyushu Island and the northern Shirakawa Barrier.

KI NO TSURAYUKI (d. ca. 945) was a co-editor of the major anthology *Kokinshū,* and his preface ("Poetry begins in the heart . . . ") is one of the most famous in all of Japanese literature. His *Tosa Journal* was a source of inspiration for Bashō.

SAIGYŌ (1118–1190) left an influential family to take Buddhist vows at twenty-three. Although he was not technically Zen, his influence on Zen aesthetics is profound. His life and work inspired Ikkyū, Bashō, Ryōkan, and countless other major Japanese poets. He spent most of his life as an itinerate priest.

FUJIWARA NO IETAKA (1158–1237) was a student of Fujiwara Shunzei. He blossomed as a poet only late in life, establishing *unshin* ("heartfelt emotion") as a major aspect of the "lofty style" that dominated literary orthodoxy throughout the medieval period.

THE PRIEST JAKUREN (1139–1202) was a monk and a nephew of Fujiwara Shunzei. His poems are included in the major anthology *Shinkokinshū*.

FUJIWARA NO TEIKA (1162–1241) was the heir to Shunzei, and he became an important literary editor, collecting and editing ancient texts including *Genji monogatari*, diaries, and a major imperial anthology as well as the eternally popular *One Hundred Poets, One Poem Each*.

ASUKAI MASATSUNE (1170–1221) was a middle-level official whose work survives only in a few poems in the *Shinkokinshū*.

DŌGEN KIGEN (1200–1253) studied in China before becoming a Zen master and one of the most influential teachers and writers in the Zen tradition. He wrote poem-sermons in Chinese verse and traditional Japanese short poems (*waka*). Five centuries later, Ryōkan wrote a number of poems by simply re-visioning *waka* by Dōgen.

KŌHŌ KENNICHI (1241–1316) was the son of Emperor Go Saga. He was a member of the *Gozan* ("Five Mountains") group of influential Zen poets in Kyoto. He was the teacher of Musō Soseki.

EMPEROR FUSHIMA (1265–1317) ruled during the late Kamakura period (1287–1298). He was a patron of poets and one of the most literate and enlightened of rulers.

Notes on the Poets

EMPRESS EIFUKU MON-IN (1271–1342) was the wife of Emperor Fushima. She was a leader in the Kyōgoku school of poets.

MUSŌ SOSEKI (1275–1351) was born to a remote branch of the Genji clan and was related to the powerful Ashikagas. His first Zen teacher was Chinese, and Musō "failed miserably." But under the guidance of Kōhō Kennichi, he received *inka* (certification of enlightenment) in 1305. He founded Tenryū Temple west of Kyoto in 1339 and worked tirelessly to preserve Zen traditions.

IKKYŪ SŌJUN (1394–1481) resigned after nine days as headmaster at Daitokuji, Kyoto's huge temple complex, denouncing the hypocrisy of monks and inviting them to talk with him "in the sake parlors and whorehouses" they secretly frequented. At seventy, he scandalized the Buddhist community by falling in love with a young blind singer and moving her into his quarters. He supervised reconstruction of Daitokuji after a devastating fire and became part of a group of artists—including Murata Shuko in tea ceremony, Sōgi in linked verse, Zenchiku in Noh drama—that brought Zen deeply into Japanese arts. The Sōgi school of ink painting was made up entirely of Ikkyū's students. He revolutionized the art of the *shakuhachi* (vertical bamboo flute).

Notes on the Poets

SŌGI (1421–1502) was a *renga* (linked verse) master whose travel journals were a source of inspiration for Bashō and Issa. His name is linked to Kyushu Island and to the northern Shirakawa Barrier.

SŌIN (1604–1682).

MATSUO BASHŌ (1644–1694) elevated haiku into great art, and his *haibun* (haiku and prose) travel/spiritual journal, *Narrow Road to the Interior,* is a major masterpiece. He made great haiku from "ordinariness," revitalized the whole critical vocabulary of poetry, and spent a lifetime searching for the "Way of Poetry."

KIKAKU (1661–1707) was a friend and student of Bashō.

ONITSURA (1661–1738) left the service of the lord of Kōriyama to devote himself entirely to the "Way of Haiku."

BUSON (1715–1783) is often the third haiku poet included (along with Bashō and Issa) in the trio that stands above all others. He was a devoted family man and successful painter.

RYŌKAN (1758–1831) was an eccentric Zen master who lived a solitary life in a northwestern mountain hut, supported only by his begging bowl. He loved the ancient poetry of the *Man'yōshū* and wrote poems in both Chinese and Japanese. Like Ikkyū, he fell in love late in life, but unlike Ikkyū, he preserved decorum except for a few poems of longing. He loved playing with children and bouncing the silk ball. In northwestern Japan, he is an authentic folk hero.

KOBAYASHI ISSA (1763–1827) was driven from his home by a conniving stepmother when he was fourteen. He lived in poverty for years in Edo (modern Tokyo), and eventually married, but within ten years, his wife and all five of their children had died of various causes. Four years later, he married again, fathering a daughter who was born shortly after the poet's death. His *haibun* masterpiece, *The Spring of My Life,* is the second great spiritual travel journal in the art form perfected by Bashō.

Meditation in Action,
by Chögyam Trungpa.

Nature and Other Writings, by Ralph Waldo
Emerson. Edited by Peter Turner.

New Seeds of Contemplation, by Thomas Merton.

The Poetry of Zen,
edited and translated by
Sam Hamill and J.P. Seaton.

The Sabbath: Its Meaning for Modern Man,
by Abraham Joshua Heschel.

Shambhala: The Sacred Path of the Warrior,
by Chögyam Trungpa.
Edited by Carolyn Rose Gimian.

Siddhartha: A New Translation,
by Hermann Hesse.
Translated by Sherab Chödzin Kohn.

*Start Where You Are: A Guide to
Compassionate Living,* by Pema Chödrön.

Tao Teh Ching, by Lao Tzu.
Translated by John C. H. Wu.

Teachings of the Buddha,
edited by Jack Kornfield.

The Tibetan Book of the Dead: The Great Liberation through Hearing in the Bardo, translated with commentary by Francesca Fremantle and Chögyam Trungpa.

The Way of Chuang Tzu, by Thomas Merton.

When Things Fall Apart: Heart Advice for Difficult Times, by Pema Chödrön.

The Wisdom of the Desert: Sayings from the Desert Fathers of the Fourth Century, by Thomas Merton.